NO MORE STATE GREENS
THE SEQUEL

NoMoreStateGreens

HUSTLE. SACRIFICE. SUCCESS.

G-FIVE
NO MORE STATE
GREENS
THE AUTOBIOGRAPHY URBAN NOVEL

#NOMORESTATEGREENS

Topgunna Promotions LLC
Published by Troy Hough
Written by Troy (G-Five) Hough
Contact: Nomorestategreens@gmail.com
Website: www.NoMoreStateGreens.com
InstaGram: @gfive_nomorestategreens
Facebook: Fivey Nomorestategreens
Cover Design by Keon Peterson @680 Media Group
Cover Design Contact: sixtyeightymedia@gmail.com
Instagram: @6080media

Note:
   Sale of this book without an official front cover may be unauthorized. If this book was purchased without a cover or a duplicate cover, it may have been reported to the publisher as 'bootlegged' neither the author nor publisher may have received payment for the sale of this book.

Copyright 2015 by Troy Hough

All Rights Reserved. No part of this book may be reproduced in any form or by any electronic or mechanical means, including information storage and retrieval system without permission in writing from the author or publisher.

For All Store Orders Please visit our website www.nomorestategreens.com or contact Via Email NoMoreStateGreens@gmail.com

Printed in the United States

NoMoreStateGreens

ACKNOWLEDGEMENTS

First and foremost I would like to give God all the praise and all Glory and Thanks for blessing me with creativity making this book possible. Thanks to my family for their loving support, my mother Harriett, my sister Eronda, my brothers Jamel & Shakeen, my Grandmother Lillie Mae and my aunt Annette may she REST IN PEACE & my uncles Gerald & Michael. To my wife Cassandra who been by my side since the day we met and never turned her back on me when things got rough I love you. To my 3 boys, Troy, Tre'jon, and Kobe y'all mean the world to me I love you guys. I also want to thank everybody that ever visited me, while I was locked up or sent me any type of mail. Special Thanks' to all that supported me on my first book NO MORE STATE GREENS without you guys there wouldn't be a NO MORE STATE GREENS (The Sequel) I love all my supporters.

SPECIAL SHOUT OUT

KEON PETERSON (aka) SpeakEazy for everything bro and my boy CHRISTOPHER SMITH... I met these two guys on the Internet and they been riding with me since day 1 #RNS. And also my entire Bagdad & TopGunna Family, Us Never Them #OnlyUs

FREE ALL MY PEOPLE'S THAT'S ON LOCK DOWN

COME HOME SOON
SCREAMING FREE YOU TIL THEY FREE YOU

REST IN PEACE TO ALL MY FALLEN SOLDIERS

ZACK, ENERGY, IKE MURRAY, KNOCK, MARLEY G, VON-DUTCH, TY-BANGA, TIZZA, BOBBIE, PIMP-MANE, PLUCK, SHAALIEE, D-RON aka THE GOVERNOR, MILTON, RAHKEIM, TWIN

CHAPTER 1

New Britain Police News

READS:

AUGUST 6, 1997

* Troy Hough, 21, of 239 Tremont St.; charged with possession of narcotics, possession of narcotics with intent to sell and possession of narcotics with intent to sell within 1,500 feet of a school.

I couldn't believe this shit once again I was back in the county jail, how the fuck I was going to get out of this one, and to make things worst Judge Scheinblum was due to return back to the bench in September. (FUCK FUCK FUCK) I couldn't sit here and cry about the situation I just had to put the (H) on my chest and handle that shit. The first 30 days was a little rough for the kid I was making a bunch of enemies, I already got it on twice with 2 different gang members, a Solido and a 20 Luv member both times over playing cards my mouth was reckless.

20 Luv originated in the Corrections

system, a spinoff of a Hartford based gang called the Magnificent 20's. The Magnificent 20's existed in the late 1960's early 1970's. Its original members are now almost non-existent. They alliances were The Elm City Boys out of New Haven and Los Solidos, but their rivals were the Latin Kings, Netaeta, and Brotherhood who were out of Bridgeport. 20 Luv had a reputation for violence to include assaults on inmates for refusing membership or disrespecting their gang. I was young and disrespectful I didn't give a fuck about none of that I was too far away from home to be acting like some pussy nigga (Na-Na PaPa) not me.

The fine I was offered was still on the table but they still wanted some jail time out of me too. The District Attorney was on some take it or leave it last offer shit, but I had to find out if my Probation officer was going to violate me first if I took a plea deal.

They offered me 18 months with a $3000.00 dollar fine, I didn't take it, I was trying to get them to put both cases together and pay one big fine so I can walk but the D.A was on his sucker shit. I wasn't trying to pay a fine and go to jail plus all the money I did have was voucher and used as evidence I was back to square one. After I refuse to take that plea offer all deals were off the table and they started to play hardball with the kid.

My next court date was dam near 2 months away in November that was way more then enough time to decide on what I was going to do.

The Hartford county jail was located on Weston Street right off of Jennings road.

Hartford Correctional Center is a level 4 facility, with a Population of 1,011 inmates, with that being 816 accused and 195 sentenced. Upon entering the system you are allowed to set up a visiting list that is sent by your counselor to those designated by the offender. The form is then filled out and returned to the facility where the inmate is being held, background checks will be conducted and it will be up to the inmate to inform the visitor that he or she has been approved. Shit was more like a Federal Prison then a County jail to me.

Since my bail was $75,000 I was sent back to dorms, D3 shit felt like déjà vu to me. I started to get my weight up doing push ups and shit because when I first got there I was only weighting like 134lbs soaking wet, I starting seeing results with in a month or so after that.
November was creeping up and I still haven't made a decision on what I was going to do, even if I did wanted to take that deal I didn't have $3,000 dollars anyway, I was dead broke calling home for commissary money.

I can't front my nigga D.P sent me a few Money Orders, and his baby mother, who is also my cousin, Smiggs older sister Karma, was accepting every collect call that came through there.

CHAPTER 2

    The morning I was due to appear in court I was awaken by the 3rd shift C.O that was on duty around 4:30am. It was pouring down raining you can hear the wind pushing the rain up against the building of the jail. I was tired ass fuck I really didn't get a good night sleep that night I couldn't fall asleep due to anxiety wondering what was going to be the outcome. I was tossing and turning all night, reading the bible and even had a few inmates that was apart of the church congregation say a prayer for me, I'm not even going to lie I needed a blessing.

    The morning sky was dark and gloomy, the clouds thundered and flashed streaks of lightening across the skyline with heavy downpour. There was a wall of water raining down you could barely see through, with those kind of thick clouds I wondered how long it was going to continue to rain with that intensity.

    The ride to the old New Britain courthouse which was located on Columbus Blvd took longer then usual due to the rain and early morning rush hour traffic, It took us about 40 - 45 minutes to get there. It's about 10 - 12 of us on the chain gang once we got there we were all uncuffed and stuffed in the same pens. Not even 15 feet directly across from us, was the females pens, them bitches was washed up tho, nobody was trying to Holla.

Just my luck guess who's on the bench (TUHH) Judge mother fucken Scheinblum! One thing about this Judge if you catch him on a good day you might get lucky the shit he be doing is unbelievable but catch him on a bad day and you're Fucked. I think he's the first Judge that started that pay a fine and promise to stay out of Connecticut for 5 years shit.

Most of the District Attorneys that worked his courtroom didn't like him he did what the fuck he wanted to. Now what's the chances of me getting that deal and for how much $$$ of a fine? Well I'm going to see today (I said to myself). I was met by a man, by the name of S. Cashmen saying he was my Defense Attorney, this nigga looked soft, I was in for a fight and I just knew I was going to lose.
The first thing I tell this lawyer to do was, try to get me a fine and a promise not to come back. I know that shit work (Facts) Smiggs got one when he got Jammed up on Oak Street, & Butter got one too back in 96 when they thought he was his brother Black and he had about 50 grams on him in a Bookbag.

Now I wanted him to run down on the Judge about getting that Fine, but this stupid motherfucker goes to the D.A with the shit. I was trying to avoid them and go straight to the Judge with my offer. If they was offering me the 18 months & $3,000 fine, "Which" they took off the table, (No More Deal) what do you think I can I get from him? "I asked!"

The D.A through some bullshit in the game and told my attorney the offer is 3 years now, plus continued my case over until January another 45 days I was pissed I didn't even get to see a Judge!!!! I was on the first go back, back to the county jail. The whole ride back I just keep thinking about them 3 holidays that was approaching Thanksgiving, Christmas and New Years and how I'm about to miss all 3 of them shit for a couple years, these crackers was on some bullshit they wasn't playing fair.

The rain had stop but the skies was still dark and gloomy. It was a real quiet ride in that Ice Cream Truck on the way back, the few niggas that did go out in front of judge Scheinblum wasn't feeling to good after that meeting he had with them. They had me in a pair of cuffs dolo; I was in a zone all by myself. I caught the count and made it back to my housing unit before Chow Time. As soon as I got back to the house niggas wanted to know " What Happen " That's how it is, niggas be on you before you even make back to your cubicle or cell.

First thing I did when I walked in the dorm was, put my I.D straight on the phones once the count clear I was getting on. You were allowed #3 15 minutes collect calls a Day and I had all 3 of mines I needed to talk to somebody and I didn't want to talk to none of them niggas. It wasn't to many people I could call, a lot of numbers I did have from NY didn't accept collect calls and on top of that your number had to be on my phone list. When I first got there I had to write every number down that I wanted to be on my phone list those were the only numbers I can call (RIFF). I don't remember who I tried to call Karma or Melly but it didn't matter, neither one of them was home.

From inside the bathroom I here the C.O calling out my name;
    I yelled out; "I'm in the Bathroom Give Me a Minute "
    My lil man come up in there like " Yo New York you got mail "

    Aiight good looking!

    It's a letter from Kay, my lil PYT from Mount Pleasant I was type shocked shorty even wrote me back, I wrote her lil ass way back in September I opened it to see what she was talking about:

LETTER READ:

Dear Gottie,

Why you lie to me???? I thought you said your name was Don Gottie? And Jay-jay seen the letter you wrote me; and rip it up I didn't have your Contact that's why I didn't write you sooner, I seen Melly and she gave it to me last week. I hope everything works out for you. Take Care!!

P.S: Write Back
KAY

I read the letter and laugh, I wasn't going home No time soon so I needed all the friends I can get. I started shaking & baking, and open up a store doing 2 for 1's, whatever I give u I wanted double back on store day or it's a late fee.
I started doing coffee balls first, niggas love coffee and they had that Maxwell House back then I was killing them, then I went to the Soups, Kool-Aid, Cakes, ETC.

My Bunky was a Lil young nigga from Hartford he got jammed up in a Town called Manchester aka Klanchester doing some wild shit, he was a cool little nigga so I took him under the Wing and put him down. We both weren't going anywhere, Klanchester had a 99%

conviction rate, they were going to get some time out you (Snapple Facts). He gave me the run down on, who owed, who took something, and who paid, shit like that storekeeper shit.

CHAPTER 3

Thanksgiving Morning

One of my Favorite Holiday mornings but this morning here I was on some bullshit and so was the C.O's. This one C.O I think his name was Edwards, I think he was from New Britain too, running around the dorm taking niggas blankets if you had more then one, waking niggas out of they sleep early in the morning. Now I'm not going to lie, I had 3 blankets it was cold in that bitch and this nigga wanted my 3rd blanket.

Now I'm on my shit; " go ahead with that bullshit Edwards I'm not giving you my blanket I need this, it's cold in here " I tells him!

" So what I don't care " Edwards said.

The inmates that came in lastnite some of them need blankets. Now I'm like I don't care either; " fuck them new niggas that came in!!! "

We going back and forth at it for a minute, long story short I give him the blanket and this nigga still tried to write me up. I got up and handle my hygiene real quick and ran down on him by the bubble,

" Edwards let me talk to you for a minute " the nigga straight ignored me!

Shit had me tight; I'm trying to talk to this nigga and he playing me. I hit a nerve when I told that nigga I'll talk to you when I see him in New Britain! I had his full attention now he, stop writing and put his pen down and stood up, and made everybody move that was around his desk area.

I already spinned off, I said what I had to say and went back to my bunk. Not even 5 minutes go pass and all I hear was
"EVERYBODY GET ON THEY BUNKS, TURN THAT T.V OFF "

Aww this bitch ass nigga push the pen! " They came in there deep looking to fuck a few niggas up; shit wasn't even that serious for all that.

They came straight to the A side of the dorm and right to my cube. They cuffed me and escorted me all the way down to the Holding Pens, that's in intake. The C.O that was taking me down to intake ran our house on the 3rd shift he fucks with me, this nigga been bringing me McDonalds French Fries for the pass couple of nights. Once he heard niggas calling me New York he ran down on me, come to find out he was from the Bronx too, Patterson Projects over on 143rd & Third Ave.

On the way to the pens he asked me what happen, I told him Edwards was acting like a Lil

Bitch, I was trying to talk to him, he didn't wanna talk so I told him I'll talk to him when I see him in New Britain just like that.

The C.O started laughing like " Yoo you crazy, that's a straight Threat you can't be doing that but that wasn't a Threat that was straight Facts that's how I was really feeling. He said he was going to holla at Edwards for me and straighten shit out, he kept his word and got me up out of there I just had to stay in there until Edwards shift was over. They riff me out and made me missed the infamous Thanksgiving Chow Meal they served at lunch time, they gave me a bag lunch with a fucking orange I was heated.

Here it is like 4 months now since I been here, in this same dorm I'm seeing niggas coming and going, some niggas even coming back. I watched this dorm flip; now it's a whole different environment from the one I walked into when I first got here. They bringing different people in here every night, if I'm not up when them new inmates get here I walk the dorm the next morning. It's 50 inmates on the A-side & 50 inmates on the B-side I slept on the A-side so I checked my side first. I gets to the B-side, that whole side flip like 3 times already so I'm going cube to cube checking shit out, I gets to the last cube in the back I see my nigga Guesss from Webster Ave sitting on his bunk. I'm hype now it's a nigga I really know from the City up in here with me. Guesss was out in New Britain too with D.P & Smiggs and got caught up for some real bullshit. It's never a good thing to see your peoples locked up but I was happy as hell to see my nigga. We walked straight to my locker I pulled out wild shit and gave it to him, food, clothes, and cosmetics whatever my nigga needed.

We started chopping it up that's when he told me his bond was only $10,000, I told him that's nothing to worry about D.P or Smiggs going to come get you out for that bond, that's lite. Like I said less then 24 hours later they was calling his name on a bond out everything I just gave him that he didn't use, went right back in my locker.

My other 2 favorite holidays came and went here I 'am turning 22 years old in prison shit just didn't feel rite.

" I'm about to spend half of my 20's up in here! " I thought to myself;

I did get a visit from my sister and baby moms they came through on Christmas Eve, that visit alone gave me the strength I needed to make it through the holidays while being locked up. It was Nights I wanted to cry and it was Nights that I did cry, shit was really kicking in I was going through it. I'm not getting the mail I'm expecting to be getting, the phone game was iffy with them collect calls, my son 3rd birthday I'm about to miss & these rednecks trying to hang me, Aww man I was (STRESS).

I'm catching ticket after ticket, Disobeying Direct Orders, Out of Place, Contraband, all kind of tickets; I even got caught inside the closet where they kept all the BIC Razor Blades. Now, I can go in there, but the C.O chick that was on duty from 4pm to 12pm didn't know I was in there.
"I tell one of them Spanish niggas to hold me down, " Bad Move Right?

"I Know!"

He lets the chick runs right up in there on me. You already know she wanted to know, what the fuck I'm doing up in there, but I think the bitch liked me tho, I was her little Tier Man she gave me the Job. I got caught red handed with it on me; It was just me and her in that room I begged her not to write it up, do whatever else you want to do to me but just don't write it up!

She was tight at me but at the same time they fucked up too, that room supposed to be locked at all times. If she reports it, then she get in trouble as well, so here's how it played out.
They made everybody lock up and go back to they cubes while they do a count of the inventory to see if anything was missing. They did the count and everything was accounted for

so we were good but the C.O chick was still a little upset with me. I was Tier Man for like 2 months any trust she did have for me went out the window. She didn't write me up either she just fired me from my Tier Man job and gave me Extra Duty.

Like 2 days later they started talking about a Pack of Razors is missing! " Somebody fucked up." Now she know I didn't take that Pack, she searched me before we left the room I only had that 1 on me. It's no way in hell she can write up a report saying she caught me in that room 2 days ago with a razor if she do that then, we all go down. They didn't know how long that room was open prior to me getting caught. They called the squad up there, to shake down the whole dorm, they were throwing niggas shit everywhere and still came up empty No RAZORS.

She never mentioned, the incident that happened with me, I respected her for that, as for them missing razors nobody knows.

CHAPTER 4

I got up earlier than usual, I been looking forward to this day for a few weeks, Court was on the schedule, it's been 5 months I been in jail now and I needed to know what's going on with my case. The morning started off good my nigga ZeKe was on deck. Zeke was one of the officers that transported us back and forth from New Britain Courts, he always looked out with the cigarettes, going to court and coming back. I used to always ask him, to cuff me by myself I hated that chain gang shit! If it wasn't crazy he looked out.

My moms had came up from the City that morning on the Greyhound Bus I was looking forward to seeing her face when I walk out in that courtroom but I never got the chance too.

The D.A continued my case again!

Just like that, another month without me seeing a Judge.

" What the Fuck going on? I asked my lawyer

" He don't want me to go in front of Judge Scheinblum for some reason I said;

" What he think's?

" Scheinblum might give me the fine?

"My lawyer replied;" He doesn't know why

" Well you better find out why; " I shouted back!

As we being shackled up for the ride back, I see the Bail Bonds Man that got me out on my last case, my man Drew. This time he was passing out cards that said 3D Bail Bonds Men, before he was working for B&B.

He said, him and his brothers started they own business along with their father! It was Don, Dan, and Drew.

" Hey Drew what would you take for a $75,000 bond? " I asked?

" Drew answered back; $5,000

Dam, 5 racks was too steep for a nigga right now I couldn't do it, I'm trying to get a fine so I can walk.

Drew told me if I run him some customers, he'd work something out with me.

As soon as I got back to the jail I put 3D Bail Bondman phone number on my phone list down at intake, now anybody that came through that needed a bondsmen I'll let them rock on my pin, they accepted all of my calls. I was sending wild flow to they business and they were coming to get niggas too. It was like a few weeks before I was due back in court when I decided to write a letter to Judge Scheinblum personally letting him know my situation, and is it anyway possible to get both of my cases ran together and pay one big fine with a promise to never come back to the State of Connecticut.

Week's goes pass, I never hear anything back from his office; by this time I'm on my way back to court. The holding pens were packed that morning; it was a lot of bodies going to court that Friday New Britain had a full house.

I remember that day February 6th that was my cousin TopBoss birthday I had just sent him a kite wishing him a happy born-day he was locked up in Washington Correctional doing 3-6 years for shooting Debo. Debo was still up to his old tricks out there in them streets playing rob your neighborhood drug dealer, he caught a few niggas too, but TopBoss put a stop to all that shit when Debo tried to rob him. I was already scheming on how I was going to get cuffed by myself, with this many people but it wasn't looking too good. As soon as they started calling out names I told Zeke call me last I'm trying to get them cuffs. No lie I get the cuffs but it's me and another nigga, somebody that's over in the pens where they hold the State inmates that's coming back down.

Guess who's the other person?   " Wop! "

This nigga was coming down on an appeal from that case he caught in 1996 he had blown trial; they gave him 10 years for that. He was putting me on how they put a crackhead on the stand that testified against him lying and shit but he had grounds for appeal. Once we get to court I started getting nervous so I pulled out my Bible, and read a few scriptures out of Psalms, I needed some more Faith.

 " Here we go again " this time it's my fucking lawyer that never showed up

" Oh Hell No " I started spazzing out;

FUCK THAT!!!

 YALL ON SOME BULLSHIT!!!

I WANT TO SEE THE JUDGE TODAY!!!!

" I'm yelling this mad loud from the pens.

The Court House is so small you can hear me from inside the courtroom I know I was loud enough because I got Scheinblum attention. He wanted to know who was making all of that noise in the back of his courtroom and ordered the Sheriff to bring me out in front.

As they brought me out, Scheinblum spoke in a tone like (I must have been out of my mind to be disrupting his courtroom)

" What is your name young man? "

" And why are you disrupting my courtroom what seems to be the problem? "

Before I even get the chance to respond the District Attorney made it well known on who I was.

Scheinblum say's " you're the young man that wrote a letter to my office requesting a fine "

The District Attorney looks over at me with a mean glare in his eyes.

I responded " Yes, Your Honor, I 'am the person that wrote the letter, I been locked up almost 6 months and haven't been in front of a Judge yet!

" Every time I come to court my case just keep getting continued, if I can get a good offered today I'll take it right now!"

He asks the District Attorney what were they offering me, now the last time they offered me anything was 3 years. The D.A says the offer is 6 Years!

" WHAT 6 YEARS " I blurted out. These crackers on some real bullshit right now!

Scheinblum then say, " Well since the District Attorney is offering 6 years

I'll make an offer of 4 ½ years, if you want to take a plea deal today. "

I declined his offer peacefully but ask him to take a look at my case maybe I can get a better offer.

" Scheinblum agrees "
And put me on the calendar for a 2 week later date.

CHAPTER 5

         I felt good this morning, I was well rested, and my spirit was up.

" Only God can Judge Me, "

I repeated to myself after saying my morning prayer while I got myself together to meet my faith.

" I had court today! "

I'm just hoping he had a chance to look over my case and come up with a better offer then what the District Attorney offered. My case was called after lunch on my way out I scan the courtroom quickly to see who's in there I might know. I then turn my full attention towards Judge Scheinblum.

" Good Afternoon, Your Honor,

He gets right to business!

" I review your file Mr. Hough and it say's here that you been busted with operating a drug den, possession of 2 firearms, and now you have been busted with some Dope! "

" DOPE! " I didn't get caught with any Dope; Your Honor!

Well here's the deal I have for you today he said,

" You can take this 7 years or 5 years mandatory!!!!

" Whoaaaaaaaaaaaaaaaa
    7 or 5 years mandatory " I replied;

My heart skipped a beat.

" He said yes, you're a drug dealer from New York City bringing that garbage up here destroying the community you deserve it!

" You need some time to think it over? " he asked

" Yes Your, Honor!

" Well have a seat in the Jury Panel and think it over! "

As I walk over to the Jury Panel it's one other person sitting inside the aisle further down on the end. I'm thinking this asshole judge was going to give me like a month to think it over; " NA-NA " more likes 20 mins. As I sits, the guy that's also sitting in the Jury Panel stands as his name is called and he goes back up there in front of the Judge.

Scheinblum must have offered him the same kind of deal and gave him 20 – 30 mins to think about it, because as soon as he got up there he whispered something into his defense Attorney ear and after that his lawyer spoke these words

" Yes, Your Honor,

" My client has agreed on accepting a plea agreement that's been handed down today by the District Attorney of the State of Connecticut.

I'm sitting there looking at this shit go down Live! I'm looking through the courtroom, they all looking at me, like

" He's not playing. "

Now I'm thinking, and I'm thinking fast too. I'm like

" Out the 7 years I have to do at least 42 months and that's if I make Parole and a nigga might get hit at the board. Either way I got to give them 36 months before I even go to parole that's 3 years."

" Now 5 years mandatory is exactly what it say it is, straight 60 months flat. It's been rumors that the law was about to change and they were taking away all mandatory sentences but I couldn't make that decision base on a rumor.

Out the 5 years with no mandatory sentence, I'll do 30 months, see Parole in 24 and I got 6 months in right now, but the shit is a rumor."

I couldn't come up with that type of decision in 20 mins and I shut down his proposal.

My case was put on the Pre-Trail docket and my next court date was set for March 3rd. That was less then 2 weeks away, they were ready to play ball but Noooooooo, I wasn't ready. Right before they came with the shackle's I saw Drew the bails bondsmen and he wanted to thank me for everything I was doing from inside the prison, he told me to give him a call tonight once I get back to the jail.

CHAPTER 6

The decisions I choses to make in life had me in the situation I'm in now, and for me trying to decide if I'm going to give these crackers 5 years mandatory of my life or 7 years with a chance of Parole was one of the hardest things I had to decide, in life thus far.

I had too face the facts, either way I was going away for a while whether I'm ready or not.

Part of my decision-making was base on the actions of my baby mother;

" I wanted to know if she was going to ride it out with me? "

When I first got with my baby moms she was just 16 years old, but that was almost 5 years ago, since then she has grown up, she hanging out now, and she like's to party. So do I think she's going to ride it out, I don't know only time will tell?

I was dam near in my 3rd dream; when I was awaken by a C.O kicking on my bunk.

" Hough you got court today you got to hurry up " he said

My day is tomorrow I tell him; I go back on the 3rd.

I know it's not my court date but arguing with the C.O about it wasn't going to change anything, I had to get up and go for that ride. We get's to the courthouse and get up stairs, as soon as I walked inside the pens, I see Pretty P, Deli and D.P little brother, B-jay! They was all in there for some bullshit cause none of their bonds was over $30,000. We were back there chopping it up for a while, I was happy to see my niggas, I been locked up a little minute now.

As usual Pretty P is back there talking big money shit;

" He's out of there less then 24hrs; He's said.

Plus he's out already on 10 different bonds!

I'm not going to even lie, niggas was looking like they were out there eating, Pretty P was fresh as usual, he had this watch on I liked, I told him;

" Let me get that watch since you getting all this money "

He talked a good one, but he wasn't trying to come up off that watch tho, he curved me.

Like I said yesterday I didn't have court but today my docket numbers is on the calendar and they were ready. As soon as I walk's in the pens they come right for me. They don't take me out to the courtroom tho; they take me to a room that have a bunch of hand me down clothes and shit. The officer that escorted me asks for my sizes and passes me a blue suit.

" Woaaaaaaaaaa Woaaaaaaaaa Woaaaaaaaaa "

" WTF is this for? I asked "

The Officer replied; you picking Jury Today put it on!

" NO the Fuck I'm not! " I shouted back; where's my lawyer? I hated my lawyer; he was letting them say and do whatever they wanted too.

I told him; " I 'am not picking no jury today and we not going to trial, let them know I'll take 4 years today! "

My lawyer returned; " the D.A offering 6 years? "

I sent the lawyer back agreeing to a plea deal that holds 5 years non-mandatory!

He returns with 5½ years last offer, take it or leave it or put the suit on. Without second-guessing I jumped right on it.

Out that 5½ I must give them 33 months, which is 50% of 66 months. I had 7 of those 33 months in already so that left me with 26 months. I see the Parole Board 6 months before my 50% and that is at my 27th month so that put me at 20 more months I got hype.

" Let's Gooo!!! I shouted; by then I should have enough programs done.

First thing I did once I got back to my dormitory, "Phone Check" I needed to get on that *JACK* Worrddd! Drew from 3D bail bondsmen left word with whoever was in that office if I ever needed a 3-way call too wherever I had the green light. I called my baby moms immediately! I let her know I copped out to 5½ years but I'll be home in 2 years on parole. I think all she heard was 5½ years because the tone in her voice changed and she just kept repeating it, 5½ years.

CHAPTER 7

I was transferred to Walker Correctional Intuition (WCI) a 4/5, high/maximum security level multi-mission facility for adult males. It was also a reception facility for inmates with sentences of 3 years or more. The facility was located in South Suffield C.T further north of the city. You're lock down for 23 hours a day, no movement and you have no property.

You only suppose to be there for 30 days or so but don't count on it, might be there longer then 2 months;

" I know I was! "

I had 5½ years as a non-violent felony and I was classified as a level 3 inmate, which mean I can go to any level 3 facilities by choice of my own. Connecticut had 21 Correctional Facility at the time of my incarceration and out those 21 facilities, 5 of them was only a level 3. My drug assessment screening was high, I was required to complete a couple of drug programs and I had to finish school as well. The thing about that was, they couldn't force me to go to school I was over the age limit where as if I was any younger

Yes they could have, but I was 22 years old at the time, I had to really want to go myself.

So now, out the 5 facilities I have to pick from at least one of them has to have one of the drug programs I needed, and I needed to be close as possible, really more convenient to NYC just in case my family members might want to come up for a visit. Now out the 5 facilities I can only pick 3 jails, and out the 3 jails I do pick, I'm allowed to pick the main jail I really wanted to go to twice.

My choices were; Brooklyn CI, Radgowski CC, Enfield CI, Osborn CI, Robinson CI.
I picked Radgowski CI as my main spot, it was right there in Uncasville, my moms knew how to get to that facility she came to visit me when I was locked up in Corrigan CI for that 30 something days, it was right across from each other and it had the programs I needed. I put Radgowski down twice and my last choice I picked was Enfield CI. I pick Enfield because I heard a lot people saying that Enfield was the best level 3 out of all 5 and it was sweeter then some of the level 2 facility plus it had both drug programs I needed and more, I'll just put those under the belt just in case.

So my list is: Radgowski CI
              Radgowski CI
              Enfield CI

Now, it's just a waiting game I was done with my 2-week assessment all I was doing was waiting to be shipped out. I waited about 60 days before my time came. I arrived at WCI in March here it is now May and I'm still here. I was praying for the day my number popped up and I was on the draft. I had a nice little journey ahead of me but no matter what I was going to make it home.

That draft day came and I was on my way!!!

CHAPTER 8

Enfield Correctional Institution

239 Shaker Rd was the address I used for the next 19 months. Enfield Correctional Institution formerly known as the Osborn Prison Farm was completed in July of 1960. It was designed to handle level 2 low-security inmates and situated on 12 acres.

Enfield Correctional Institution received its first inmates in 1962. These inmates worked the surrounding farmland until 1986. During the fall of 1987; the population was increased from 420 to 724.

In June of 1991 the security was raised to house level 3 and level 4 inmates. In October of 1993 the facility was made a level 3 medium-security facilities as it remains today.

Ever since that riot back in 1992 that erupted after a dispute over a carton of cigarettes and a bag of drugs that left 13 injured, the facility made a few changes on how they ran things since then. 11 inmates out of 250 inmates that participated were charged fingerprinted and arraigned in an Enfield Superior Court and returned to various state prisons.

As soon as I get there it's a problem, my property is not on that bus. Now I'm tight, I need my Tim's they had me rocking these karate Joe slippers for 2 months already I needed my boots, plus all my clothes and cosmetics' I stacked up while sitting in Hartford, my food, my mail with all my pictures in it and my Walkman. I spoke to a couple of Gold Shield Lieutenants and they all told me the same thing

" Give it a few days if your property still doesn't get here, come back and see me "

For 4 days I'm walking around this compound looking like a bozo, like I don't have peoples out in the world that love me, before my property finally get to me;

" I'm feeling like a New Man Now "

" Now I could Diddy Bop through this shit, the

way I want too! "

Enfield was the sweetest spot; this place was wide open; you had to walk everywhere just to get somewhere. It was movement all day long, go where you want to go. You could run around in different buildings, your cell was your room we had our own key!

The yard was crazy; it was about 400 niggas out there. The compound population was only 715 inmates at that time, so that was a little more then half of the Jail out in the yard. Niggas is out there fresh; all types of flavor sweat suits on. I got right in the groove, I had a few sweat suit too mama luv sent up, while I was in the county jail. I took that state shit right off, only time you had too wear the pants was in the mess hall, school or for visits. My construction Tim's was still crispy I felt so much comfortable.

My Bunkie peeped it " feel much comfortable right " he said.

Hell yea much better, now I can start my Bid!

My Bunkie was a nigga from Hartford name D.C we pulled up together in transit, he was leaving MacDougall CI a level 4 facility, his level had drop so he was being transferred to a level 3 and so was I. Son was a cool funny nigga, he was the first nigga when I started writing rhymes I let hear me spit;

" Nigga straight lied to me and told me my shit was hot "

I spit some trash to that nigga that day, I know it was trash because I had gotten much better in due time. I had run into D.C 4 years later in another spot and I spit some bars for him and we both laugh because we both remembered when I first started rapping.

D.C was the first person I started fucking with in that spot, he gave me my first Sidney Sheldon book (Master of the Game) I ever read, I was hooked on Sidney Sheldon after that, I read all 23 books he wrote. Up there, it was a town thing, Hartford niggas stuck with Hartford niggas, New Haven stuck with New Haven, Bridgeport stuck with Bridgeport, and New London fucked with New London.

" I'm a New Yorker, so I fucked with my New York niggas. "

I don't care where you at it's always a New York Nigga somewhere. Like this one kid I met name Blondie; he was from the city too, Davison Ave, in the Bronx's.

" That was right there; couldn't get no closer to home then that. "

I told him where I was from and he knew everybody from my hood.

I started to go to school while I waited on that long ass waiting list for this Tier 2 Substance Abuse Treatment Program. Tier 2 is an evidence based curriculum driven treatment program provided three - four times a week in a non-residential setting. Tier 2 helps the offender develop an understanding of addiction, triggers and relapse prevention and how addiction has affected the cognitive, physical, social and familial spheres of their lives. Tier 2 also helps offenders identify and plan for the educational, vocational and consumer based issues they may face upon release.

It wasn't a got dam thing wrong with me I just needed that shit for parole, fuck all the bullshit and politics' about it. I needed to get back in school anyway I never finished, I got kicked out of William Howard Taft High School in 1993 when I was 17 years old, that was 5 years ago I haven't been to school since then. I was smart in social studies, science and math but I couldn't fuck with that Algebra shit or write an essay so I had to work on that. I was only a few credits from getting my Diploma when, I decided not to go back.

My moms even signed me up for Job Corp I dubbed that shit tho; they try to send me all the way to Kentucky (FOH).

CHAPTER 9

" Hough you got mail " C.O Jackson yelled out;

It's about time sheesh! I had been waiting on a piece of mail for the longest, finally! It's a letter from my baby moms.

It read:

July 9, 98

Hello Tray,

How are you doing? Fine, I hope. I know you are surprise to hear from me. The reason I'm not coming to see you August 19th, I forgot you're visiting days. You have to tell me again. I knew one thing when I came, I should have a new hair style. Please, listen to your facility rules & regulations for my dress code. You have to tell me because that's very important to cause I don't want to travel out there and we to make a u-turn. You know what I'm going to try. I'm going to try getting my own apartment in 10 Belair Gardens. Right now there's one thing I have to get off my chest because it's killing me inside for lying to you, peace. You been in jail. I had a friend a Puerto Rican friend but he look black. The good thing about it I did not have sex with him and I not with him. I wasn't feeling it. I did not feel right messing with someone else that a reason why I wasn't writing you because I

Here it is, I only been down 11 months on this 5½-year bid and I get a fucking; " Dear John Letter! " Hearing your name being called during mail call is like a special feeling you get to keep you motivated, but them Dear John Letters is one piece of mail you pray you don't ever get. I haven't receive a letter from my baby moms since I left Hartford back in March and now I'm standing here reading a fucking Dear John Letter. Our relationship was already on shaky grounds due to some false accusations one of her girlfriends said about me, but this letter confirmed it, it was over between us. This was the last letter my baby moms ever wrote me and also the day she officially stop being called my girl into being called, The Baby Mother.

I was fucked up in the head for a couple days I really didn't know how to deal with it; but I had to accept it and let it go. I really couldn't focus on doing my bid without thinking about what's going on out in the real world. I was on the jack 4 times a day and that shit just made it harder for me to accept it. Once I got to D-Building, I started to run into other nigga's from New York like my son Napo from Brooklyn and that nigga use to see me going through it on them phones. One day he just told me;

" Leave them Phones Alone and do your Bid "

As soon as he said it I knew what I had to do. I'll be having a good day chillen, but as soon I get on the phone that shit will fuck up the rest of my day. I didn't stop using the phone but I did stop calling her, the next time I did pick up a phone to call her was December 31,1999!

CHAPTER 10

It was a new year and I was really focus, I just completed that Tier 2 program I needed, I signed up for Tier 3, I'm trying to get my High School Diploma so I can graduate in June and I see the parole board right after that in November! I still had a long road ahead of me but at least I wasn't looking uphill anymore, I was looking down. I started putting on some weight I gained a few more pounds and I grew dread locks. I just spent my 22nd, and 23rd birthday in prison hopefully the 24th will be the last one. As I'm getting older, so was my son he's 4 years old and I was missing him like crazy. I was chillen tho, when I wasn't in the yard catching some air, I was right there in the dayroom playing poker or watching B.E.T that's how my days went.

It was a Wednesday morning; (French Toast Day) I got up for breakfast like 5am that morning and walked to the mess hall. It was Napo and me as usual the last 2 niggas to leave the building as we get to the mess hall I see the nigga Pretty P sitting at the table!

" Oh Shit, what the fuckkkkkkk is upppp!"

Last time I seen this fake Pretty Fly nigga, he curved me on that Watch, back in the county jail, I didn't forget about that shit " I just spoke to his peoples and they told me he was over at Robinson CI, that jail was right down the street from where I was at. I introduce Napo to my nigga Pretty P.

" I see they finally caught your ass, " I said to him.

Pretty P had gone on the run for a few months after he pleaded guilty to like 10 different charges he caught out in New Britain before they caught his ass. He had bounty hunters all in the hood out in the Bronx's looking for him.

" See nigga, You should of gave me that Watch I could have been putting that shit back on your wrist Right Now."

We finishing chopping it up before we left, we was the only 3 people that was still in the mess hall besides the kitchen workers, I told Pretty P I was going to come check him at 8:oo am once the count clear.

" Fuck school today I'm not going " I said to my cellie! My nigga Pretty P on the compound!

My cellie was from New Britain too, he knew who Pretty P was, my son Groove from Mount Pleasant. Groove told me him and Pretty P had a little disagreement when they were both out in the town and he didn't really know how Pretty P was still feeling about it. Groove was my nigga too, plus we been cellies for 6 months, so I had to make sure I deaded that shit from the gate.

Once Pretty P finished up his Orientation phase he signed up for school and came over to D – Building with me, and we eventually became cellies a few months right after that. Shit felt crazy, we was just kids, ten years ago running around playing baseball now we both in the same jail, with 11½ years between us both sharing a cell together. Pretty P coming to Enfield helped my bid out a lot, but it was headache's that came with it. Pretty P was my childhood friend but to everybody else on that compound including Captains, Lieutenants, and Sergeants, he was my cousin. Pretty P had the same type of attitude I had when I first came to jail but that was almost 2 years ago I changed since then, I was growing up, but this nigga stayed in some shit especially with the C.O's every time he did something they was calling me with the shit. I was ordered 1 time to keep him out of trouble or I was going to have to answer to that.

When P first got to Enfield he only had 5 months in, he was still smelling like the streets I was trying to school him, I been down 18 months I knew the ropes. The good that came out of Pretty P being in Enfield with me was, I finally got a chance to see my son who I haven't seen in 2 years.

The visiting schedule was Riff tho how everything was setup with the even and odd number day.

There are no visits on State Holidays (New Year's Day, Martin Luther King Day, Lincoln's Birthday, Washington's Birthday, Good Friday, Memorial Day, Independence Day, Labor Day, Columbus Day, Veteran's Day, Thanksgiving Day and Christmas Day.

- Visiting policy is based on the Odd/Even number system, where the Inmate's last digit of his institutional number will coincide with the date (Odd or Even date).

  It seems liked everywhere I went Pretty P wasn't far behind we were always getting into some shit together, so of course when I first got my Department of Corrections Din Number for the state of Connecticut he also got his Din Number.

  My Din was #250***

  Pretty P Din #250***

  I had an Even Number and Pretty P had an Odd Number we still made it happen. Since I was from out of state I was allowed Special Visits, which allowed me to have a visit on a day that was Odd. Pretty P girlfriend who was from the city, Nia, whose is also my son Godmother, brought Troy-Troy up to come see me on a visit when she came to visit Pretty P her and her girlfriend, China! China was my nigga Short-Man girl, we all grew up together just on different blocks. Short-Man was locked up too, but in New York State and he still showed me love by letting his girl come up with Nia to bring my son, not too many niggas would have done that even though China could beat that little nigga up, it was a respect thing. I was very Thankful for that. Pretty P was out of control, but he was focus, we both graduated in June 1999, and received our H.S Diploma's.

    Around the time Pretty P came to Enfield so did Def Squad recording artist Keith Murray. Keith had caught 3 Years for an assault case while preforming a show in New Britain C.T, somebody got their head bust at the show that night and he caught the blame. The day Keith Murray pulled up to the spot he had the compound in a frenzy, it looked like the whole jail was in the yard that day. Keith was a cool nigga tho, once he came to D-Building we got real close. Like a day or 2 after Keith came to D-Building right after chow niggas was up in the bathroom smoking when Keith walked in, shit went from a blunt cipher to a rap cipher real quick. Everybody that was in there started spitting, I'm not going to front I wasn't going to spit but my nigga Grundy from New Haven called me out. I spit the best rhyme I had that day and Keith liked my flow and told me to just keep writing. He gave me some pointers on how to write 16's and hooks, we recorded 2 songs together and before you knew it we was preforming for the inmates in the jail.

For our Graduation Ceremony Keith Murray preformed;

" The Most Beautifullest Thing in this World "

For all the inmates and family members that attended the Graduation.

" Shit was lit! "

I didn't have anyone from my family come up but I did have 1 person that wrote me to see how I was holding up in there, surprised me and showed up on Graduation day to show some support, another childhood friend of mines Brandi. To this day I still respect her for that, and No we wasn't secret lovers or nothing like that, just friends that grew up together and hung out on the same block.
It felt good to stand up and receive my High School Diploma, I finally accomplish something good, but it wasn't over just yet I still had my Tier 3 program to complete and plus I see the Parole Board in 5 more months. I been Ticket free since I left the county jail I was just praying those didn't come back and bite me in the ass. (No Freaky)

CHAPTER 11

After the graduation, I was done with school, so I got myself a job, working inside the laundry room in my housing unit. The laundry room was a gold mine, we was open 24hrs a day, three 8-hour shifts. I had the 4 – 12 shift I was bringing in close to $250 a week in commissary, I was charging niggas $2.00 a bag some people $3.00 if you wanted your clothes washed. We had recreation 3 times a day, some niggas worked out, played basketball, softball, volleyball, tennis whatever, all-day everyday, every rec and they wanted their shit washed everyday, and if you wanted a speedy process might cost you a little more.

My moms and sister had came to visit me when I first got here, but after that visit I told them that they didn't have to come anymore I'll be alright, ever since then my moms just sent packages. I was waiting on a package my moms were supposed to send me 2 sweat suits, and some boots, so I called home to see what's going on. My little brother Melvin Sleepz answered the phone & the first thing he said was;

" Yo you gonna be Tight my Nigga "

Why, What happen; I said!

" Mom brought you a pair of Sketcher's; And she already mailed them off. "

" WHAT!!!!!!!!!!!! " I said;

    I was on Fire I was not wearing no mother fucken Sketchers, not this New York nigga. I needed them Black Chukka's not them stupid looking space boots. When they called me down for my package I told Sarge to send them shit right back, don't even open them I had a different pair coming in the mail.
    Pretty P & I were good we didn't need shit, our lockers were to the capacity with food and cosmetics; we had a T.V and a Radio. Some nights we took turns cooking depending on, if we wasn't both at the poker table gambling. Every Sunday I did the cooking tho I couldn't afford for Pretty P to fuck that chicken meal up, it was either going to get Curried or Barbecued. We had the mean kitchen connect that brought us whatever we needed, Onions, Pepper's, Garlic, Curry ETC. I also ran the Football Pool; money was coming in all ways. The only nigga that did hit my tickets was Pretty P, but he never got paid. For the next couple of months I just finished up all my programs I had to complete, I even completed 2 Anger Management classes just in case those county jail tickets haunted me.
    Now I've been waiting on this day since March 3rd 1998 the day I copped out to these 5½ years; my date with the Parole Board. I have

never been so nervous like this a day in my life I just kept thinking to myself why shouldn't they give me my freedom back, I did everything that was required for me to do and more.

" If I make parole today I can be home in 6 more months, " I thought.

That's around May, right before the summer time; I got hype!

CONNECTICUT BOARD OF PARDONS & PAROLES

PAROLE ELIGIBILITY INFORMATION

By statute, offenders who are serving a total effective sentence (definite) of at least 2 years and 1 day are eligible for parole consideration.

Parole eligibility is calculated at 50% or 85% of the total imposed sentence (less any jail credit). Risk reduction earned credits awarded by the Department of Correction can also reduce parole eligibility for non-violent offenders only (50% designation). Current convictions and/or criminal history will determine the designation.

Each hearing consists of three board members and a parole officer. Inmates are allowed to express to the board why they believe they should be paroled, the Board then asks a number of questions. Once these questions are complete, the Board convenes in Executive Session and returns to give the inmate the decision.

I went in there and let them know why I deserved to be giving a second chance, I was very remorseful for what I've done not only to me but also to my family and I showed them I use my time wisely by continuing to further my education by receiving my High School Diploma. I also completed both Tier programs 2 & 3. I waited outside while they decided on a final decision whether I should be release or not. I sat outside and prayed and prayed and prayed and within 15 minutes my faith was decided and I had a date May 7th 2000!

I'M GOING HOME........

CHAPTER 12

I was going home but that's in 6 more months, anything can happen between now and then that's when niggas really start to act up, they know you not trying to lose your date. My level been dropped I was a level 2 inmate for a few months now but I made the facility put a hold on me until I completed my Tier 3 program. Them Level 2 Facilities was trash if it was up to me I'll stay in Enfield until it was time for me to go. I was eligible for a Halfway House Work Release Program so I sat down with my counselor and filled out the paperwork.

Work Release: Programs designed to provide assistance to offenders in obtaining meaningful employment. Offenders reside in these programs for an average of 4 months under 24/7 on-site supervision. The goal upon discharge is for each offender to have stable employment, an acceptable place to live, and sufficient savings to live independently. Program staff assist offenders with needs such as obtaining identification, developing a savings plan, obtaining a GED, developing a resume, finding employment and securing housing. CTDOC holds contracts for 696 work release beds around the state, 50 of which are reserved for female offenders

I didn't get to pick which halfway house I wanted to go to I was only allowed to pick a district. It was 5 different districts to choose from;

Bridgeport, New Haven, Hartford, Waterbury, Norwich.

I picked New Haven for a reason because when I went in front of the Parole Board since I wanted to be paroled to New York City they mention that it can take longer and I can be release anytime after May 7th. My best bet is to apply for a halfway house and find someone address I could parole too, then transfer my parole over to NYC.

Special K and her mother Thelma had an apartment out in West Haven, they told me I was more then welcome to parole to their crib. Thelma and Special K was doing good for themselves, Thelma been clean 4 years now and Special K went back to school and finished up her education and now works as a tax paying citizen. Special K and Melly always kept in contact with me I was like they older brother. My nigga Black came home and him and Melly was doing good as well.

I was told I had anywhere from 45 – 90 days before the Halfway House accept your paperwork once it's sent out to the district, it was like an lottery pick, one big business trying to pick the best candidate. I estimated the time frame, which I should be out of here right after the New Year!

CHAPTER 13

New Years Eve 1999

      This was one of the biggest, New Years ever we were bringing in, The New Millennium (Y2K) and it was on a Friday. I woke up feeling like something good was going to happen today I just had a gut feeling. I put on one of my newest sweat suits my Navy Blue joint, with my all white high tops with the gray swede check, Nike uptowns. I only wore those on the visit, I didn't have too many of those so these joint were icy white I kept them in a bag. C.O Ms. Jackson & Ms. Mitchell were both working D Building that morning I think that was the real reason I got all-fresh in shit and I even through some of my smell good on, I liked Ms. Jackson little ass but Ms. Mitchell was my bitch.

  I'm inside the dayroom chillen watching SportsCenter on ESPN when Ms. Jackson walks in with a big grin on her face.

What you smiling all crazy for Ms. Jackson? I asked

Her next words were, PACK UP!!!!!!!!

I repeated it; " PACK UP are you serious where I'm going? "

I been on this compound for 19 months and today I'm on another draft but this time I'm halfway home I was on my way to work release.

The Roger Sherman House in New Haven Connecticut accepted me. We were allowed to wear our own clothing, smoke cigarettes freely, and use the phone as many times as we wanted too and also, I was finally able to listen to Hot 97.

The Roger Sherman House is a male work release program designed to re-integrate into the community, ex- offenders who are productive, successful and law-abiding. Achievement of this goal is facilitated by employment placement, the development of suitable housing, and reduction of risk through interventions targeted to address criminogenic needs.

The night I arrived at the Roger Sherman House, I put all my pride to the side before the New Year came in and made that call to my baby mother, we haven't spoken to each other over a year, plus I wanted to talk to my son, Lil Troy birthday was coming up in a few weeks he was turning 5. The plan was, for me to find a job and stack my paper for the next 127 days, everything was going accordingly to plan, up until I got denied from being paroled to Special K and Thelma crib. I was stacking my chips and I had 2 jobs that 127 days I thought I had to do, flip to 188 days real quick. I had 30 days left when they hit me with that bullshit, it was to late in the game for me to give them a New York City address now, plus the process was going to take at least 4 – 6 months. The next best thing was for me to get another address before the 7th of May, or get my own Apartment which, that wasn't a problem, I've been working 2 jobs so I had the money I just needed the crib so I started apartment hunting just in case.

At the Roger Sherman House they made us open up a Bank Account and every week once we got paid we had to deposit our whole check inside our account. I had a job working at Stop & Shop and Au Bon Pain. I landed the Stop & Shop job as soon as I started job hunting; it was only part time so I was allowed to find another part time job working in a bakery. The pay from Stop & Shop was bullshit $6.45hr but I didn't give a fuck I was just working up in Enfield for $24.00 every 2 weeks; I worked any extra hours they gave me that's how I made my money.

Stop & Shop was litt, all kinds of females working up in there on them cash registers. The halfway house had about 61 niggas in there I was tired of being around niggas all-day, now I was surrounded by pussy. My baby mother & I were done with each other so I was free to do whatever I wanted too. One day I had to leave work early I wasn't feeling too well I had a sharp ass pain right near my Navel by my upper Abdomen and I had a Fever of 102 degrees Fahrenheit. I couldn't eat anything all day, once I started vomiting, I told Staff and I was taken to Yale Hospital. At first, staff tried to send me back over to Whalley Ave; to the New Haven Correctional Center and have the department of corrections medical staff run some test to see what was wrong with me. I didn't want to go back to the county jail just to sit in the pens all-day and hear the same results, that it's nothing wrong with me, I needed some real medical attention and not from them toy nurse's over in New Haven CC. Once I got to Yale they ran some test and discovered my appendix was bad. I was admitted and told that surgery would have to be performed for the removal of my appendicitis.

Appendicitis is an inflammation of the appendix, a 3 1/2-inch-long tube of tissue that extends from the large intestine. No one is absolutely certain what the function of the appendix is. One thing we do know: We can live without it, without apparent consequences. Surgery went well and less then 24hr after surgery was completed I was being discharged, due to the way my medical expenses was set up Yale New Haven Hospital made it clear I over stayed my welcome. A couple of days on bed rest and a prescription full of Percocet's I was right back on my feet again.

CHAPTER 14

Apartment searching wasn't like going out shopping for an outfit I was real picky I didn't want to live just anywhere I had to be real cautious, New Haven aka Elm City wasn't one of the sweetest towns in America.

In 2000, New Haven had the highest murder rate in Connecticut (14.6).

This rate was higher than the rate in four of the cities — Boston (6.83), Denver (6.04), Pittsburgh (10.52), and San Francisco (7.73).

Murder Rates in Five Connecticut Cities, 1990 - 2000

Cities	1990	1991	1992	1993	1994	1995	1996	1997	1998	1999	2000
Bridgeport	40.9	35.9	40.3	43.8	36.6	24.8	33.1	25.6	23.1	21.8	13.6
Hartford	13.6	17.2	9.3	22.7	41.7	26.6	16.1	16.9	18.8	15.9	14.0
New Haven	23.8	26.0	23.0	17.8	25.8	17.6	18.4	17.6	12.0	9.7	14.6
Stamford	9.3	9.2	6.5	7.4	5.6	3.7	5.6	0.9	2.7	2.7	0.9
Waterbury	4.6	8.3	11.0	18.7	7.5	8.7	12.6	7.7	6.6	2.8	11.2

In 1999, New Haven had the lowest murder rate in 10 years but the statistics shown here in 2000 it was back on the raise again. I found a studio apt over on Division & Mansfield Street, most people called that location, The Ville section of Elm City, for $450.00 a month I liked it but the parole officer had to approve the area first before I can even drop a deposit. It took about a month for me to even find an apartment; a lot of them landlords wanted to do a credit check, and once I did find a decent enough spot the parole officer took an extra month just to go approve the shit. Here it is now July and I'm still sitting in this funky ass halfway house I was ready to go. I had a few racks in my account I put the first month and the security to the side, the only thing I needed next was a bed I been buying a few other things here and there. I started putting that phone pressure on him calling the parole office complaining to his supervisor, a few times of that and I had confirmation to be release in 48hrs.

    I was finally a free man, but for how long was really the question. First thing I did was after I had my furniture delivered was, go see my parole officer and right after that I jumped right on that Metro North headed to New York City. Not even 8 hours of me being released I was in violation of my parole already. For 36 months I had been playing this scene out in my head but now it's finally happening I didn't know how to act.

    The block was the same just a few different faces, a lot of the young niggas grew up, they was on the block now. My grandmother was still living in the hood back then, I surprised the hell out of her when I knocked on her door, she couldn't believe it. I had put on some weight, my face was all-fat in shit, I was a grown man now but I was still her grandbaby. I made my rounds through the city seeing all of my family before I had to go back home to Connecticut I had to work the next morning, I already used one of my sick days I couldn't keep calling out, I was officially on my own and had bills to pay;

" Welcome to the real world!! "

CHAPTER 15

<u>NoMoreStateGreens</u>

Living in New Haven was kind of stressful for me, I was happy to be free but I was alone. I didn't have any real family members or friends out there with me. I did have a lil shorty name Shay from out there that I was fucking with, I met her working up in Stop & Shop, she was one of them cashiers I mention earlier but shorty was going through her own little issues with her baby father. Shay was 2 years older then me, born and raised in New Haven her whole life, she knew that town like the back of her hand. She had 5 other younger sisters whom I became very close with in due time, they treated me like a brother anything I needed they was there for me.

Shit got rough once my Stop & Shop checks started getting garnish;

" Back Child Support Payment! "

Those bastards started taking $87.00 a week out of my checks, and I was only getting paid $6.45Hr working 4 days a week. I needed more hours badly, I started working 7 days a week 40 – 60 hours just so I'll have enough money to pay bills. I was a part-time Produce Clerk working full-time hours, most of the time I was in charge of the 4 – 12 shift. I use to come to work some days at 1pm and didn't clock out until 12am, I had rent I had to pay, Light & gas bill, public transportation and I had to buy food for the house I wasn't getting any food stamps I was going hard.

I reported to my parole officer monthly so on the day I was due to report I put in a request for a transfer back to New York. I knew the process was going to take at least 120 days, I'll just continue to keep working until the paperwork goes through.

When Thanksgiving, Christmas and New Years came around I felt like I was still in prison I couldn't spend none of the holidays with my family or friends due to me having on an ankle bracelet.

Ankle bracelet) is a device that individuals under house arrest or parole are often required to wear.

The most common configuration is a radio-frequency transmitter unit that sends a signal to a fixed location-receiving unit in the offender's residence. The residence unit uses either a landline or a cellular network to relay information to a service center computer. If the offender is not at the residence at times stipulated, an alert message is sent to the service center, and then relayed to the supervising probation or parole officer.

I got locked up out in New Britain one nite with J-Dog, the nigga had a warrant & when they pulled us over they found some marijuana paraphernalia in the backseat. It was J-Dog car so he took the charges and we both was release on a PTA (promise to appear). Part of my parole stipulations was, No Police Contact so once I got arrested I had to let him know. When I went back to court I was offered 10 days community service, which I declined quickly for 2 reasons;

#1 I was just a passenger and that paraphernalia was found in the backseat,

#2 I didn't smoke weed I was on parole!

The case was dismissed but I still had this fucking bracelet on, I couldn't move how I wanted to, up until the lights in my apt shut off. Ever since I put in the paperwork to be transferred back to NYC I stop paying bills, fuck that I needed every dime, I even stop paying my rent.
No Light, No Electricity that also meant no working service computer. I was due to go back to parole in 2 days, my timing was off 72hrs, I was hoping by the time I go back to parole my transfer was ready. I get's inside his office, and my parole officer tells me my paperwork has been lost we have to start the process all over.

"Fucking unbelievable " are you serious I said;

Connecticut Light & Power just turned my lights off & I stop paying rent about 2 months now, but

I didn't tell him that part, hoping my paperwork was ready. Luckily I was having this ankle bracelet remove today because then, that would have been another issue.

It was over for that crib I was out of there, I wasn't about to pay 3 months of rent and Connecticut Light & Power, I packed up everything I needed and bounce. My home girl Special K had her own crib now out in New Haven right there in the Ville on Read Street so I stayed with her. Special K been living in New Haven only for a few months and was trying to find another apartment back out in West Haven closer to her Job. She only moved to New Haven because her baby father was from there, but since he went to jail it wasn't any need for her to stay anymore. I stayed with Special K for about 2 months up until she was ready to move. I could have moved with Special K out to West Haven but I didn't want to commute, Public Transportation ran on a funny schedule at night out there and I got off at 12am. I moved in with one of Shay sister's Nobia out in Amityville off of Whalley Ave. Nobia was wild cool she let me stay with her for a few weeks up until I had to report back to parole.

The whole entire time I been on parole my P.O never did a home visit but today as I'm sitting in his office he tells me he's going to come by my crib tomorrow morning. I couldn't lie, I had to be straight up and tell him the truth, I wasn't staying on Mansfield Street anymore, and

I got behind on my bills so I moved out. My P.O wanted to know;

" Where I was staying and who I was staying with! "

That was the problem; I really didn't have an answer. I told him whom I was staying with at the time but I couldn't stay there long because Nobia daughter father was using that address for himself to parole too. He gave me a week to get my shit together before he put me up in YMCA. The YMCA was like a 3-quarter house for parolee's that violated certain stipulations or didn't have an address to parole to. I stayed in the YMCA for 30 days until I was able to come up with another address. Shay got me an address staying with one of her other sisters that had a house out in Fair Haven on Chatham Street. Shay and I had a bugged out relationship, she still was living with her kids father so I was the side nigga.

I started to get real home sick, I wasn't happy anymore living in New Haven, I had no family or real friends out there, even though Shay family treated me like family, I didn't feel right about it so I decided to leave and move back to New Britain.

CHAPTER 16

I found a 2½-bedroom apartment over on Union Street, my nigga Mista-D hook me up he knew the Slumlord. I had my Parole transferred which only took about 2 weeks to do, I was still going to be living in C.T, and my job; Stop & Shop had many stores through out the state. New Britain was like my second home I felt real comfortable living out there maybe a little to comfortable because I started to slip.

Most of my homeboys were still out there, so niggas still had the town. Black came home and got rite back in the mix, it was him, P.O.P, K-Lou and Mista-D, the rest of my homeboys like J-Dog, Butter, D.P, Pretty P and Smiggs they were all locked up. J-Dog just got snatched a month before I even got to the town, Pretty P was still doing his 6yrs, D.P had 4yrs, Butter was doing 5½ and Smiggs had 3½ yrs, they had to extradite Butter and Smiggs both from New York.

Now I was still working but I'm not getting the hours like I was getting down in New Haven, I'm barely getting part-time hours, my checks is still being garnish and I have rent that needed to be paid plus I was running out of money. When I moved to New Britain the only stuff I traveled with was my clothes, any furniture I did have was left back on Mansfield Street, I had to start all over. This time I went with the Rent-A-Center bedroom set with a couch and a T.V, and that was an every week bill.

Moving to New Britain was the first sign of me going backwards, this was the same town that gave me 5½ yrs., which I was lucky enough to even make parole, but yet I was back and slowly but surely I was back to my old ways. It wasn't no more, sitting up in trap houses waiting for customers to come, call my phone, and I'll come to you that's how I was on it. Before J-Dog went to jail he gave my nigga M.J the green light to come out there but the day after M.J pull up J-Dog got knocked. When M.J pulled up he brought his whole family with him, his baby mother, his son & her daughter they were 4 deep and stranded, and couldn't go back to N.Y for whatever reason. They were staying with some of J-Dogs peoples that lived out there for a little while, but things got sour and they put them out. Now I always been a good nigga it's just in my blood to do for other's anyway I can, so when I heard my nigga M.J needed a place to stay we just split the rent on the 2½ bedroom apartment.

Everything was running smooth up until 1 day I came home from work and as I'm coming through Union Street I spotted the Narc's in front of my house. As I rode pass, I looked up and seen that they were inside my apartment from the Window so I kept it moving. About a week prior to that incident them same Narc's had raided the apt under us, some Spanish people crib. We never sold any drugs out of there but a few people did know we lived on that block but that night they raided the apartment under us I had a gut feeling they hit the wrong crib that nite. As they were on the second floor we was coming up the steps once we walked pass, they all look at each other confused. From that day, I just kept telling myself they was coming for us I didn't know who sent them, maybe the people downstairs sent them, I don't know, but they was on to us. The day they raided us the Narc's had seen M.J riding thru the Plaza, snatch him up and brought him back to the crib, they didn't have a warrant so they couldn't knock the door down. They didn't find anything but a few pictures that confirmed that I lived there so I knew they were coming back next time with a warrant. I couldn't stay there no longer I packed up and took flight I was not waiting around for them to come back fuck that crib, fuck Rent-A-Center, fuck parole, I'm gone New York Bound.

2 weeks before my birthday I turned myself into parole I wasn't with that running shit you have to have money to be on the run and I wasn't trying to catch a new case on top of that. I called my Parole Officer while I was down in the City and explained the situation and told him I couldn't no longer stay in that town I wanted to go back home to New York. I had about $1600 dollars when I turned myself in I had to make it

last for these next 13½ months just in case I had too max out 2-5-2003. My level went back up so I was sent to a Level 3 facility; Brooklyn CI out in Brooklyn CT. I hated that spot I was trying to get back to Enfield CI, but they was sending all the violators up here, this spot was for sex offenders, the only thing that spot was good for was good T.V reception. First thing I copped was a color T.V, a Walkman, a sweat suit, thermals, underwear's, and cosmetic's etc. I was scheduled for a parole hearing within 30 - 60 days of returning back to jail. February 2002 I went up for my parole hearing and was reinstated after 90 days. During the hearing the parole board mention the reason of my violation, which was I couldn't maintain my living stability, so I asked can I be paroled straight to New York City since I had no immediate family members here in Connecticut.

March 7, 2002 was the day I was due to be release on parole but since I was paroling back to New York City it might take awhile longer so it was anytime after that date. I was transferred immediately to a Level 2 facility I had never been to one; I left from Enfield CI a Level 3 facility when I went to the Halfway House back in 1999. Waiting for New York Division Of Parole was a hell of a wait. I waited 5 months just to be told that the address I gave them was denied, I had already been through 5 different facilities when I got the news. Once I left Brooklyn CI I was sent to Gates CI where D.P & me were in the same dorm together for a little while, then I was transferred to Bergin CI, got into some shit over there and got shipped to Willard-Cybulski CI, where I sat in the box for a week before being release and shipped over to Osborn CI. Once I got to Osborn CI, they put me in the same house with Black he was back on a Violation, Butter and K-Lou pulled up too while I was there, before I went back to Gates CI. My second time around through Gates CI, P.O.P & me were together in the same dorm for a few months before him and me both were transferred and I was sent to Garner CI. New York was playing games I supposed to been home ever since March, it's now July and I'm just hearing from these cocksuckers. I run down on my Counselor and give him another address but I also sign up for a Halfway House if I have to wait another 5 months I'll wait in there. All I was doing was waiting around playing poker and watching B.E.T videos, Rap City The Basement was my shit. I couldn't wait to go home, put back on some real clothes and take this state shit off. It was looking good for a couple of niggas from my hood in the rap game; my nigga Bali was in the Source Magazine Unsigned Hype Colum and my nigga Hell Rell was signed to the Diplomats.

Around the 2nd week in October the Johnson/Silliman House on Retreat Ave before it became a women and children's program that offers a continuum of services designed to prepare female offenders for transition back into the community, accepted me for work release. I landed a job working at another Au Bon Pain in St Francis Hospital for the remainder of my time. 2 weeks before I was due to max out New York Division of Parole notified me saying my new address has been approved I told them sons of bitches

" Go suck a whole frank stand "

I've been waiting on y'all for the pass 10 months, I go home in 2 weeks I don't need parole now and hung up!

It was now 2003, I started this journey back in 1996, and finally it was almost over I traveled before, but this was one hell of a trip. I was 20yrs old when I caught this case, now I'm 27 and I'm just getting my life back. I spent most of my 20's in the penitentiary, I grew up in there, I had too or I might have been lost. Prison can do 2 things to you and that is, it can either; Make You or Break You and I wasn't about to let it break me. I thank God for giving me the strength to be strong-minded and helping me get through all this. I wasn't fortunate like most people that were visited by family members and love ones I had about 10 visits my entire bid but I did receive a lot of mail. What a lot of people fail to realize is

You don't have to drive up and sit behind a table
"You don't have to send money if you're not able"
"Send a kite, just to see if I'm alright."

    That's one thing a person in jail will always remember, it doesn't have to be a long letter, even if you write a one-page letter that shit will get read about 4 - 5 times. I really want to take this time out and thank everybody that took 10 - 15 minutes out of their time & 75 cent to see how I was doing I appreciated it.....
    I got lucky and was release 5 days earlier due to Corrections closing down the Johnson-Silliman House and sending inmates to different work release programs within the town.

CHAPTER 17

Troy-Troy was now 8yrs old, I went to prison when he was 2, I missed all the potty training days, first days of school, Graduations, all because of poor decision making. I couldn't get that time back I just missed; I just have to do the right thing now. I was a Free Man, No Parole, No Probation, No Programing, No Nothing.

I was back home, in the Big Apple, the City that never Sleep. My baby mother and I were officially done with each other so I had to move back in with mama luv. I haven't live with my moms since I was like 7 years old shit felt funny to me. My moms had move down to Harlem back in 1997 when I first went to jail, to Wagner Projects. I was born in Harlem, but I never lived in Harlem I had to get use to it, I was a certified Bronx nigga. It was a full house up in there I had to get on my job.

The hood was still the hood, we lost a few good men through out the years of my incarceration, Monster-G was killed back in 2000 and First & Last was killed in 2002. My nigga Jumpa and Dirty Red was still out there, Topboss was back home off that 3-6yrs, Mizzal was on the Island doing a bullet in the 6 building, and all the rest of my niggas I came up with was in Jail too but the game didn't stop, it was a new breed of hustlers out there holding the block down. All the young boys that use too play in front of the buildings we hustled out of was now official block hugga's, they were deep too. When I first came home I wasn't really press for money but I wasn't sitting on no racks either, I was only working for 90 days how much can I have stacked. Hustling on the block wasn't even in my thoughts when I came home, and I was dam sure, I wasn't going back out to Connecticut selling nothing, I was just chilling I really didn't have a plan I was just getting the feel of New York back.

While I was locked up on my Violation Shay kept in contact with me here and there, not like how she supposed too, even though I didn't expect her too, but she did reach out. I waited almost about a month before I called her and let her know I was even out, shit the way she wrote me, it just showed me how much I was on her mind, so I felt it really didn't matter to her if I was home or not. My relationship with Shay when I was living in New Haven was; I was just her side nigga, everybody in her family knew I was fucking with her, but not anybody else, which I could respect & understand because when we first met she was still living with her baby father, but when she finally moved out to a place of her own, she still denied our relationship, acting like she was scared to be seen with me by her baby father, shit like that. Well I was wasn't with all the sucker shit so I bounced, we was still cool tho, one nite her and her sister Nobia drove down from Connecticut to come check me. I wined up riding back with them all the way to New Haven, staying the rest of the night and I just jumped back on the Metro North later on the next day. This time I was done with Connecticut, New York was my home, my city and we had a lot of catching up to do.

CHAPTER 18

    The summer of "03 was approaching and I was dead broke, I needed some money! I been home for 90 days and that little bit of money I came home with was gone. I been hanging out in the hood ever since I been home, and niggas was eating out there. The hood had wild love for me I had the green light to do whatever I wanted too; I can't say the same about anybody else but I wasn't no stupid nigga that was just going to jump right back in the game with his eye's closed, I had to sit back and watched what was going on I haven't hustled in the hood since 97. I had to learn all the fiends first before anything and then all the undercover D's unmarked vehicle's that was riding around. The 46th Precinct they didn't play fair, so you had to be on your A game.

    The 46th Precinct is located in the central part of the western Bronx on 2120 Ryer Ave. The area includes four neighborhoods known as Fordham, University Heights, Morris Heights and Mount Hope. The commercial strips are along East Fordham Road, Grand Concourse, West Burnside Avenue and Webster Avenue. The precinct consists of both residential and commercial areas. The 46th precinct played real dirty, they had this one cop at the time named Porky, him and his team were beast, when they hopped out somebody was going down. I needed some money but I wasn't ready for the game just yet. The block was hot and it was about to get hotter. One of the young boys from the hood got killed, the lil homie Taz (sleep in peace). Taz was a little getting money nigga, he wasn't with all that beefing shit, he got killed down the block over some other niggas beef, some niggas came through they set blowing shots at them niggas, and Taz got hit fucking with them. Then on the same night a few hours right after that my nigga Dollars got shot, the hood was on fire.

While I was incarcerated I went to church here and there but I believed in God and made sure I read my bible all the time and prayed every night. God knows my heart, I believed that every thing he put me through was a test of my faith and too make me a stronger and wiser person. God must have seen I was about to head down that road again and bless me with a job. My lil bro Melvin Sleepz got me a job working with him up in Yankee Stadium as an outside vendor selling hot dogs, pretzel, and soda. The pay was bullshit I could tell you that off top, we got paid off commission 10% off every $100 the more we sold the more money we made. Hot Dogs and soda's were both $4.50 each, them Yankee fans didn't give a fuck about the prices they brought us out. Lil bro & me started scheming, we was turning in $1000 - $1500 a night to these crackers I needed that type of chicken for myself.

My brother found a spot uptown in the Bronx's in co-op city that sold the same hot dogs we was selling in Yankee Stadium in a Sunoco gas station. They sold us a box for $40, 2 packs came in the box. These were Hebrew National Foot longs, no supermarkets in the tri-state sold these trust we looked all over. 20 – 23 hotdogs came inside of 1 pack and I had 2 packs, so that's 23 x 4.50 = $103.50 + another $103.50 it was time to eat. Most of the time 20 came in a pack I was still good with that 20 x $4.50 = $90 cash so that was $180 off 1 box that was exactly $140 profit I was making at that time, shit was better then buying grams.

    The company I worked for inside of Yankee Stadium was called Centerplate. Centerplate Inc. is a food and beverage corporation serving entertainment venues in North America, and the UK. Centerplate was formerly known as Volume Services America, Inc., and was originally a division of The Flagstar Companies. They supplied us with every thing we needed if you left the warehouse with $2000 worth of food and beverage's you was responsible for that bread your math game had to be up, no time to be counting on your fingers with a line full of people waiting, it was cop & go. Depending on who the Yankee's were playing determine how many packs of hotdogs I took from the warehouse. My normal I'll take was 5 packs unless the Mets or Boston Red Sox's was in town then that's a different story, I'll need about 10 packs just for starting. From 4pm until the game is over and the crowd is gone I'm out there selling food. From the 3rd inning until about the 7th inning is straight down time you'll probably get a few customers here and there but most of the fans are already inside watching the game. If I sold all 5 packs by the 3rd inning that I took from the warehouse, I wouldn't ask for a re-up I'll just replace all 5 packs from my stash and pocket the $450, niggas was even doing the soda & water game buy a few $1 waters or soda's and sell them for $4.50

    It was all kind of hustling schemes going on out there, you had the scalpers with the Tickets, nigga's selling Yankee's hats, and kids selling candy you even had the homeless out there with the why lie I need a beer sign! Everybody was eating, we wasn't the only one's scamming the company, you had supervisors, security, the vendors that sold souvenirs, plus every vendor that worked inside the stadium that sold Beer, Cotton Candy, Popcorn, Dippin' Dots Ice Cream or Cracker jacks had a hustle, even them chick's that was on the cash registers was rapping them blind. I finally had a legal hustle, well it wasn't really legal, I just wasn't going to jail for it, the most I'll get is fired, I didn't give a fuck, for that chicken that's the chances I took. It was most definitely a hot summer in NYC that year every chance I got when the Yankee's weren't in town I wasn't either. I was all over, spending money; enjoying my freedom I felt I owed that to myself at least. It was a weekday in August my people's asked me did I want to ride out with them to Virginia Beach for a couple of days; I was with it.

Not even 24 hour of us being down there when we turned on the T.V to

Breaking News: **Northeast blackout**

The **Northeast blackout of 2003** was a widespread power outage that occurred throughout parts of the Northeastern and Midwestern United States and the Canadian province of Ontario on Thursday, August 14, 2003, just before 4:10 p.m. EDT. Some power was restored by 11 p.m. and many others got it back two days later. At the time, it was the world's second most widespread blackout in history.

Major cities affected

City	Number of people affected
New York City and surrounding areas	14,300,000
Toronto metropolitan area and surrounding areas	8,300,000
Newark, New Jersey, and surrounding areas	6,980,000
Detroit and surrounding areas	5,400,000
Cleveland and surrounding areas	2,900,000
Ottawa	780,000 of 1,120,000*
Buffalo, New York, and surrounding areas	1,100,000
Rochester, New York	1,050,000
Baltimore and surrounding areas	710,000
London, Ontario, and surrounding areas	475,000
Cambridge-Kitchener-Waterloo, and surrounding areas	415,000
Toledo, Ohio	310,000
Windsor, Ontario	208,000
Estimated total	55,000,000

Some people might have looked at it as just a power outage but not everybody felt that way, some people even called it the **2003 Blackout-Bush Conspiracy?** The timing was way too convenient - just days to weeks before crucial votes on Bush's sweeping energy plan and Clear Skies Initiative - both designed to dramatically over empower and expand the fossil-fuel-driven electrical power generating industry. If 9/11 got G.W.B the Patriot Acts, why shouldn't a massive power outage get him "Energy Acts"? The timing of the blackout was too coincidental. It occurred just weeks before Bush plans to shove a sweeping energy plan through Congress that will not only force America to be ever more dependent on fossil fuel for decades to come, but will turn the American electrical utility system into a giant megacorporation sans competition, sans recourse by consumers.

It was chaos for the evening rush hour in NYC, Commuters had to sleep on steps, hitchhike or walk home as trains were powerless. That's a New Yorkers' worst nightmare the power going out while you're in the subway, and you get stuck on a train in the dark with hundreds of people. Then above the surface New Yorker's is dealing with gas pumps that stopped working; food spoiled as refrigerators and freezers thawed; jugs of water sold out as supply plants lost their ability to supply consumers; The Brooklyn

Bridge looked like a scene out of a post-apocalyptic movie hundreds of people walked across the bridge to get in and out of Manhattan. By day 2 of this Northeast Blackout people started seeking shelter wherever they could find it, some people literally slept in the streets of Time Square during the blackout.

As the summer was coming to an end so was Baseball season the Yankee's had 41 regular season games left with 23 of those were home games it was time to start stacking chicken for the off season.

CHAPTER 19

These past 7 months since I've been home has been the longest I ever lived with my mother, before I went to jail I lived with my baby moms but since we parted ways that lead to the results of me going back home to live with mom dukes. My mother loves me so she didn't mind not one bit, she was happy to have all her kids home together all under the same roof. My moms might have not had a problem with it but I did, for one I felt I was to grown to be living at home with mommy and for #2 it was too dam crowded. I have 2 younger brothers and they kept some company coming through there I couldn't do me like I wanted too. One day I was just sitting in the house thinking about my next move when I get a phone call from Shay. I haven't spoken or seen her since her and her sister pulled up on me in the city a few months ago. I was type surprise to even hear from her, she never calls me! At first it was all small talk, up until she hit me with the

"I'm Pregnant" shit!

" WHAT! Wait a minute what you just say "

" I'm Pregnant she said:

I heard her the first time but I had to make sure I wasn't too high hearing things that wasn't said. She gave me the whole run down on how her monthly didn't come this month or last month all I could do was SMH. Of course off top I asked her was it mines, shit I didn't know what she was doing out there. I admit tho, I did go skin that night and (Shot up the Club) I was bugging. I was not ready or financially stable enough to be having any kids and I was living with my mother no way. I explained to her that, it was not a good time or a good idea to be having a kid especially with the predicament I was in. She took it as a sign of disrespect and did what she wanted to do and once again I didn't hear from Shay until February of 2004 when my son was born. By that time I was already out of mom dukes crib in a relationship and living with my lil shorty I bagged working inside the stadium. I always use to see shorty and her crew coming through the bleachers on they shit, they was apart of that scamming the company for a couple dollars too.

My brother Melvin Sleepz knew one of them her name was Beania and shorty invited us on a bus ride to Sesame Place for her son birthday, once I found out that all them chick's from the bleachers was going I was in there. Sesame Place was Litt I had never been there before, this was my first time; I had never been to Great Adventures either up until a month before that. When I seen Beania one day at work I let her know I really enjoyed myself but I really wanted the run down on one of her friends. I told her which one it was, and she said her name was

Cassy. I liked shorty style she was wild cool and laid back. Shorty wasn't looking for a nigga to take care of her, she had her own money. She was single with a 4-year-old son, with her own crib just her and her sister, they shared a 3-bedroom apartment.

Right before the last couple of games before the regular season ended I ran down on Cassy and we exchange numbers. From the gate I was straightforward with shorty and told her my situation that it was a possibility I was having a seed. I told her we weren't together and plus, I haven't talking with her in months so it wouldn't be a problem. On the Off Season after the holidays and the new years passed, Cassy and I used to just travel out to Virginia like twice a month and stay a whole week if New York got bored to us. For the first 2 times, we did the Greyhound thing but after that we couldn't take it anymore I went and got my license and copped me a whip.

The first car I brought was a 1999 burgundy Ford Contour I caught that at a dealership auction upstate in Newburgh NY. For Valentine's Day Cassy and I drove out to Virginia for the weekend, V-Day fell on a Saturday that year. We left New York City Thursday morning, that same night I receive a text saying Shay had the Baby, she named him Tre'jon. I love my son to death but I always felt in my heart that Shay must have thought by keeping the baby, that was going to make us be together, but it was too late for that. I didn't know how long my relationship with Cassy was going to last but the few months we've been together so far, I was enjoying myself it felt good to have a girlfriend, I been lonely for a few years.

CHAPTER 20

    For the next 5 years I just continue to scam Yankee Stadium by selling my own product on their property making money on the side. Baseball season was only 6 months long, depending if a team made the playoff or not. So from April – September I always had a job but from October - March I was out of work. During the off seasons I did fall back into my old ways getting my hustle on selling crack in the hood, I just wasn't going that hard I had no plans of getting rich on that corner. I was stacking all my chips I was making at the stadium for the off-season so I wouldn't have to hustle, but it just wasn't enough to hold me over, them holidays & birthdays played a big part. I managed to stay off Riker's Island without catching any felonies, that's the good part, but I did catch a few Misdemeanors charges, mostly all for Marihuana, central bookings was the furthest I went.
    I needed something else to do with my time so I got into this music business. I didn't know shit about the business all I knew was how to write rhymes and format a song, I just remembered what Murray taught me. I got tired of going to other niggas studios paying $25 – 40 dollars an hour; so I brought my own equipment all I needed was a computer and Protools. I

started up my own label and signed myself, Bagdad ENT with my niggas Top Boss & Casino Brown. I didn't need any handouts, I recorded my own music and did my own promotion, I just used different social media outlets and flooded the Internet with music. The era I grew up in if you wanted to make it out the hood you either had to have, a wicket jump shot or you slung crack rock. Well I wasn't a ball player so I slung crack rock, but now we had a new lane to make it out and being an artist in this hip-hop industry was the way. I seen it happen with my own eyes, my nigga Hell Rell made it, he got signed to Diplomats Record and now had his own label Topgunnas Entertainment. Hell Rell and me go way back we grew up in the same neighborhood we just lived in different building but we slung crack on the same strip. We all had our own running's with the law that lead to us both taking incarcerated vacations. He was about to get signed right before he turned his self in to go back up-north back in 2002, Cam'ron kept it 100 and waited for him to come home and the rest is history. He was doing him and I was doing me we were bound to cross paths one day we were on the same road.

One day my nigga Big Bill hit my line and told me to pull up on him, he was over there on 148th & Brook Ave up in the Bronx's by Zoo Studio's. When I pulled up, Big Bill & Hell Rell was parked up in a whip blowing on some Cali Kush, Rell had that Black spaceship back then, that 745 BMW, I parked the lil hoopty I had and jump in his shit. Rell was putting out a Mixtape call The Extermination: Return of the Grind, he was trying to get that shit done ASAP but he needed an Engineer. We drove out to Jersey, my nigga Duke Da God had the studio out there and went too work. That same night J.R Writer came thru and they recorded a track called DeathWish. That tape had 19 tracks on it I recorded 12 of them. I was out of work so I had nothing but time on my hand, that Yankee Stadium gig was up, that 2008 season right before they tore it down and moved across the street, they fired all the outside vendors. Doors started to open for me I started learning more and more about this industry, everything was viral. I brought a camera and started recording everything behind the scene and launch BagdadTV on YouTube along with TopgunnaTV.

      After losing that Yankee Stadium gig, I just fell back and focus more on this music, I wanted to win but it wasn't paying the bills. I really had to get on my job once Cassy found out she was Pregnant. My relationship with Cassy was still going strong, we had over 5 years in, and we were way overdue. I kept my promise and went out and found a job. I landed that job at the right time Cassy was due to give birth in November. My people's I went to Taft H.S with Snoop got me a spot working as a Building Superintendent at a Family residence shelter. Snoop and her brother Boo had management under the wing, both of them was running their own buildings. Like I said not even a week after I told Snoop I needed a Job they called me. Cleveland Family Residence was a Homeless Shelter just for females with a child 3 years old or younger at the time. I was the Head Super in charge of all maintenance and repairs for 15 apartments, that's 33 rooms I was responsible for.

CHAPTER 21

Kobe Qu'ran Hough came into this world December 1, 2009 at 10:32pm inside of Jacobi Hospital. I didn't witness the entire birth but I was there the whole time I didn't leave the room. I just can't stomach certain shit, like all the blood and mucus, that shit just look nasty, it felt like I was going to faint, my knee's started getting weak on me. I learn something new that day about females, when they giving birth most of them have the tendency to remove their bowels.

The New Year's was approaching and it was looking like I was finally walking that straight path, I was officially done with the streets. I fell back from the hood, the building superintendent job I had was working out well for me I didn't have to hustle anymore I just focus more on this music shit. I still had my Bagdad ENT label but I was more focus on this Topgunna movement, even though Dipset had broken up Hell Rell still had a buzz in these streets so he was the main focus. We put out a few Mixtapes that I featured on like:

(Bullpen Therapy, You Need People Like Me: The Return of the Black Mask, Million Dollar Dreams Federal Nightmares, and Us Never Them)

We recorded The Extermination: Return of the Grind in Duke da God studio but all the above mixtapes was recorded in my studio. We rocked a lot of shows off them mixtapes. Rell was the rapper so they paid him to perform I made my money by booking shows and features for him I was the contact. I managed emails accounts, websites, productions, and promotions. I was using every social media I knew to network.

      I worked for Bryant Housing Partners for 2 years before being fired in December 2011. Now that was crazy, I got fired for some shit that happened on my day off. We had this one client that was just out of control she just did what she wanted too. She had a problem with every staff member on each shift including most of the other clients, I wrote her up at least 40 times. So on my day off she got into it with a few other clients in the kitchen area where she almost caught the smack down if one of my co-workers didn't interfere. She didn't like me, everybody knew that so she decides to calls (DHS) Department of Homeless Shelters and tell them she was in fear for her life & I tried to get her jumped while she's pregnant, and they believed that shit. Every female in that house was Pregnant I couldn't understand it plus I wasn't even on duty. I was called in the next day for a meeting, which really wasn't a meeting it was just to tell me I was fired.

CHAPTER 22

For the past 2½ years I worked as a taxpayer citizen, I woke up everyday by the grace of god and went to work but today shit was different I didn't have a job. Christmas was in 19 days and I still haven't finished my Christmas shopping for Troy-Troy & Tre'jon. I smoked about 3 blunts while I contemplated my next move. I haven't sold crack for 3 years but once a hustler always a hustler you never lose that touch so that wasn't the problem. I really didn't want to go back to the hood unless I had too. My nigga Bigg Bill was doing his thing on 148th and he gave me the green light to come eat over there. I already knew some of the customers plus Bigg Bill had this one fiend name Kacey who ran us all the money from his building. My first day out on the block my nigga Bigg Bill put me on to this 1 customer he had coming through from Long Island Queens this chick name Dez copping numbers, she spent a straight $600 with me, I gave her 63 bags. From that day on I was officially back in the game I didn't know it then but my life was about to make a change for the worst. Shorty definitely didn't look like a smoker so after I made the sell, I ask my nigga Bigg Bill where he knew her from and how long he been dealing with her? Bigg Bill tells me he just really started dealing with shorty directly, she was Kacey peoples, he been bringing her through. I didn't think anything else of it I just kept doing my thing.

After the first couple times Kacey brought Dez through everything went through him now she didn't need him anymore she cut him off and started calling the trap phone direct. 2 days right after Dez spent that $600 with me she was calling again for another 30 bags that was $300 I hit her with 2 extra. Dez really wanted some weight but around that time the streets was drying up, prices was high and you had to be careful a nigga didn't give you some bullshit or rob you. As for me getting Dez some weight that was out the question I was making a better profit off her then I would if I was putting 3-4 points on the gram. We was bagging up $100 a gram, so if you was spending $300 I was bagging up 30 bags that's 3 grams. Coke prices were between $36 – $42 dollars a gram you do the math. The money was good, kind of to good to be true Dez came and seen us 6 times in the month of December alone, she spent over $3000 with us.

For my 36th birthday, Hell Rell had a show booked out in Bridgeport Connecticut on Christmas Eve so I invited the whole gang to come out and party with us. We drove out there 6 cars deep, shit was Litt and we brought about 15 bottle's inside the club with us. I really had a good time that night that was one of my best birthdays thus far I really enjoyed myself. I'm not the club type of person that like to party every weekend, you might catch me in a club here and there but that's only on special occasions;

celebrating one of my people's birthdays. Plenty of times Rell and Bigg Bill tried to get me to come out with them to the club's and we was getting in every spot free Mobbin, I still wasn't with it. After a while them niggas just stop asking me, they already knew the answer. The only time I did hang out tho, when it was show time and show time only. I'm not going to say I don't like to club because I do I just don't like to party if I don't feel comfortable. If I have to be in a club watching niggas every move I'm not enjoying myself, that's just me. I think I just, kind of, out grew the party scene, I been partying since the house party days. I did the Fever, Savoy, Parkside Plaza, Rumba's, Cherry Lounge, Club New York, Club Envy, Octagon, Shadow, I was in every spot that was popping. The only club I never had the chance to go to, I heard so many stories about, was the Tunnel I missed that era.

CHAPTER 23

2012

    The year started off looking real good for me, I was getting a couple of dollars, and I was chillen. Dez was still coming through and right after the New Years she started to step her shit up. I smoke a lot of weed so I tend to get paranoid most of the time, so when I notice the increase in money she started to spend I got nervous. First thing that came to my mind was (The Police) I brush it off tho, I just thought maybe it was the weed or it could have been I just was feeling that way because I haven't been in the game for a while. As soon as the year started, it was like the 4th of January, Dez called the trap phone and said she was coming through & she wanted 200 bags she had 2 racks. The day she called I just so happen to have the trap phone in my possession Bigg Bill usually speaks to her and I meet up with her and make the sell. I don't even have 200 bags I tells her, I only have 150. At first she was hesitant on even buying the 150 from me, she claim she had to talk to her people's and see if they would split the 150 down the middle 75/75. Dez was getting money out in Long Island selling heroin and had a few customers that wanted some rocks too, so when Dez came down to the city to Re-up she brought a few bags and started pushing them for $20. That shit kind of fuck me up when she act like she didn't want the 150 bags. The Coke prices was funny plus a lot of niggas wasn't holding the streets was dry, I let her know if she was going to come for it I'll hold it down for her. Once Bigg Bill pulled up in the hood I let him know about the conversation I just had with Dez.

    Bigg Bill has been my nigga for over 15 years prior to this conversation. Bigg Bill was originally from Cortland Ave, he have a sister name Sweet T that moved to my hood back in 1994 -1995. Once Bigg Bill started to come through, it just so happen that he knew my nigga Dirty Red and they linked up and he stuck around. I met my nigga Bigg Bill around the same time 94-95 we both slung crack together on the same corner, and we both slung Orange Bags. Both of us been in this game a long time so, we knew the rules (never sell to anybody you don't know) but neither one of us really knew Dez, Kacey did. That same nite Bigg Bill ran down on Kacey, G-checking him on where he knew Dez from. Kacey was from Harlem; he was a getting money nigga before he got hooked on his own product, now he was living in the Bronx's still chasing that first hit. Kacey said he knew Dez older brother before he got killed Dez was his people's he swore up & down she was good his story was convincing enough because we kept serving her.

    For the entire month of January Dez came through 3 times on the 4th, 12th, & 26th, and spent a total of $5500 with us each time she came she spent $2000 except for the time when I only had the 150. Even though Kacey vouched for her who's to say he wasn't lying, so I started to test Dez out. One of the times Dez came through I shorted her just to see if she was going to complain or not, she did and when she pulled up the following date she asked about her extra's I shorted her on. I really wanted to serve her some fake work but I didn't want to lose a good customer.

Super Bowl XLVI weekend New York Giants vs. New England Patriots. The Giants ended with a 9–7 record during the regular season and returned to the playoffs for the first time since 2008, winning the **NFC East** and finishing the season as the NFC's No. 4 seed and The Patriots finished with a 13–3 record, winning the **AFC East** and clinching the AFC's No. 1 seed in the playoffs. New England lost 2 consecutive games to the **Steelers** and Giants in week 8 and 9 respectively, before rallying to win their remaining eight games. I'm a big Giants fan so you know I was rooting for Big Blue. The broadcast of the game on **NBC** broke the then record for the **most-watched program** in American television history, previously set during **the previous year's Super Bowl.** Super Bowl XLVI was watched by an estimated average audience of 111.3 million US viewers, and an estimated total audience of 166.8 million, according to **Nielsen**, meaning that over half of the American population watched at least some of the initial broadcast. Well out those 111.3 million viewers I wasn't one of them, I was sitting up in central bookings.

That Saturday morning Dez called my phone and tell me she's on her way down and she needed her regular 200. The streets were dry I didn't have any work, Bigg Bill either but I didn't let Dez know that. She called me early that morning I didn't have much time I had to move quick. I went to my hood to see if I can get my hands on something real quick, when I got over there my nigga Mizzal was the only nigga out there, it was like 10:30AM. He was out there busting all types of moves in and out the building; it was a little flow coming through that morning. As we chopping it up the flow just kept coming and during that wave of customers TNT (Tactical Narcotics Team) was out there observing. Every sell Mizzal made was inside the building so they couldn't see shit they just waited until the customer came out and ran down on them. They hopped out on a female customer and in her possession she had 2 bags of crack cocaine. They had the customer now they was coming to pickup the dealer, Mizzal peep the van rolling down the block and dipped inside the building and disappeared on them dickheads. They were tight they didn't even know which way he went so they snatch me up and charge me with Criminal Sale of a Controlled Substance 3rd PL 220.39 B Felony. The female customer and I were the first 2 inside the pickup van; we rode around for 4 – 5 hours before they took us to the precinct. They were determined to catch Mizzal but they were a minute too late, he was long gone but they hung around the hood anyway. They sat there and patiently waited and it paid off when they collard my nigga J.B and caught him in possession of 60 bags and mark money. They didn't get who they really wanted but they were more then satisfied with J.B instead. When I got to arraignment I was charged with Criminal Sales, Intent To Sell, and Criminal Possession. They didn't find a bag or any mark money on me so I was ROR release on own recognizance that Monday evening after sitting over 48 hours in them pens. That following Tuesday I made it my business to file a Civil suits against the 46th precinct for Unlawful Arrest. I hired a Lawyer by the name Vik Pawar, (Pawar Law Group P.C) to handle the case.

    I was home for 9 years when I caught this felony but this case was bullshit, they didn't have any evidence, I just had to deal with the back & forth to court shit, I wasn't copping out to anything. The plan was to get this case dismissed and then sue.

CHAPTER 24

Tre'jon 8th birthday was 2 days away on the 12th of February when Dez hollered at me. Dez timing couldn't have come at a better time I wanted to get Tre some more stuff before I mailed his package off to him. Shay wanted a new start from Connecticut so she moved down to Richmond Virginia, she wasn't alone 3 of her sisters were already living down there so she was good. Shay had let Tre come stay with me over the summer but I didn't get to spend as much time like I wanted too due to work, I was working from 4 – 12 but I did get the chance to take him to Dorney Park. Bigg Bill moms had through a Bus ride that summer and I took him and Lil Troy, Kobe was still a baby.

That 2 stacks Dez spent with me made everything work out nice. This time when I met Dez I told her to meet me at the Wendy's on Third Ave by the Cross Bronx Expressway. After I made the sell, I started to get a funny feeling about Dez, was it paranoia, I don't know but I do know 1 thing I stop serving her and I changed my number. I fell back from 148th and put some work up in Edenwald Houses, uptown in the Bronx's I had some peoples up their pushing packs. That worked out for like a month or so before I decided to take my hustle back out of town.

      Hard Hittin New Britain here I come! As soon as I mentioned it to Cassy she wasn't with it, first off she didn't even like the fact that I was hustling, now I'm about to go out of town (Sheeesh) I went through it with her. My nigga Black and his lil brother Butter, had the crib on High Street, niggas already said I could come through, whenever I was ready. Black drove down to the city and picked me up so on the ride back we was chopping it up and he was putting me on about the town. I haven't sold crack in New Britain for dam near 10 years if not more but yet I'm back. I still knew the town and how to get around so that wasn't a problem for me, all I had to do was stay out the limelight. First thing I did was buy me a pre-paid trap phone with a #860 area code and gave out the number. I ran into a few people I knew and let them know I was back in town; I had to show my face. At first I was just running around with Black shaking moves, he use to leave me his phone and the car keys at night, he knew I wasn't trying to go to sleep and miss any money #TeamNoSleep I was straight Vamping.

      Within 2 weeks I copped my own whip, I Brought a 1991 all White Cadillac Coupe Deville from some old couple in Farmington that posted the ad on craigslist. I love old school cars especially Cadillac's I had to get it. These last 4 months was the longest I went without having a G-ride. I sold my Volvo back in November to the junkyard, that's exactly what it was "JUNK". I spend more money on that car then what I paid for it. One thing about me I always kept a G-ride tho, that Volvo was my 4th car since I been home, I had that car for about 2 years before I finally sold it. I always wanted a Coupe Deville; I use to tell my nigga G-man (R.I.P) that shit all the time. We stayed at them Dealership Auctions trying to catch one for the low low we couldn't score for shit. Now I finally had my own, all I wanted was for my nigga to see I finally got one. Before I had Butter fix me up with the Insurance & Registrations I gave it, its first real test run, I shot down straight to the city. If it could make it to the city and back with no problems it's a keeper. Butter let me use one of his license plates from off his other car and I drove down, I had the Lil homie Skrapp with me.

New Britain still was popping that town was full of money and it was enough to go around for everybody. Niggas phones were ringing so much; niggas wouldn't serve you if you had less then $50 unless we were out in the streets already making moves. Black or Butter wasn't jumping in there cars driving anywhere for $20 - $30 dollars. Within no time I was back in my groove, up & down that interstate. The coke prices in the city was still high as hell but I didn't care the comeback was crazy.

One day I was just sitting up in the crib on my Smoking & Thinking shit, I had a 8th of some sour on the table but I was low on Dutches. As I'm smoking I just started thinking about hitting the Lotto leaving all this shit behind. Here it is 15 years later and I'm back. We hop off that Greyhound Bus 6 deep back in 1994, in 1996 I was the 250,596 person to go through the Connecticut Department of Corrections and it took 7 years just to get my life back I thought by now I'll be done with this lifestyle. I walked over to this gas station on Farmington Ave call Sam's, to buy a box of dutches, but before I even order the boxes of dutches I try my luck on a Mega Million lottery ticket. The Mega Million was worth $640 Million all I needed was $2 and a dream. I brought 5 tickets I'm going try $10 and a dream. If you ever notice all lottery winners mostly win from a ticket they brought at a small mom & pop store or gas station and Sam's was privately owed. As always I let the machine pick my numbers, now all I had to do was wait, the drawing was at 11:00pm. Winning the lottery was like finding a needle in a haystack, what were really the odds of me winning 640 million well we would see tonight. My ticket read:

A. 02 04 30 43 46 MB: 23

The numbers drawn Friday night in Atlanta were
2 – 4 – 23 – 38 – 46 Mega Ball 23.

After seeing I had the first 2 numbers, my heart skipped a beat I started to get excited but my dreams were slowly crushed when the next 2 numbers read 23, 38. I even had the 46, and

Mega Ball # 23, I was close but no cigar. I still won but it wasn't anywhere close to that 640 million, for having 3 numbers plus the mega ball I was awarded $200 if I would have had 4 numbers plus the mega ball that was $10,000.

    The end of the month was always slow I was just trying to finish and Re-up before the 1st. I been grinding all weeklong my body was shutting down I needed a goodnight sleep in my own bed I couldn't wait to get back to New York.

CHAPTER 25

MAY 2, 2012 3:30PM

Baby wake up! The Police at the door! Those was the words coming out of my wife mouth that snap me right out of my dream into my worst nightmare of reality. As I got up & went to the door, sure enough in my hallway stood 7 New York undercover detectives from the narcotics division squad. The first thing that came to my mind was that these dick heads is at the wrong apartment, but little did I know they weren't. As much as I hate to admit it, the Tactic's the police department use's to apprehend a suspect without a warrant is very cunning. Before I jumped into this drug game, I was taught 2 main rules that I lived by which is #1 (Never sell crack where you rest at) and #2 (never get high on your own supply), so not at one time did I think that the narc's that was at my front door was there for me. They started out asking me a few questions, they wanted to know my name & know who else was in the house besides my wife & me. I told them my government name & let them know that nobody else was there beside my wife and me, and my 2-year-old son. After telling them my name I was asked to show some identification. I told my wife to grab my I.D out of my wallet and bring it to me. I was then asked to step out into the hallway; I didn't see anything wrong so I did. After being properly identified I was place under arrest and charged with 10 counts of criminal sells of a controlled substance 220.41.

    This has to be a dream I thought to myself as I stood in the middle of 7 Special Narcotic Detectives on the ride down in the elevator of my building.

" I just got back to the city this morning, how the fuck I fall asleep and wake up to this shit, this can't be real. "

When I came to the door all I had on was a pair of Olas Basketball Shorts and my R.I.P G-man T-shirt, them niggas tried to violate and take me to the precinct dress like that. Luckily wifey was on point and grab my sneakers and my hoodie. I was taken to the 40th precinct on 138th Alexander Ave in the Bronx's. As soon as they walked me inside the precinct 10 – 15 minutes later they was bringing in Bigg Bill.

    They drove us down to Manhattan 100 Centre Street all Special Narcotics cases was being handle by Special Narcotics Prosecutor,

Bridget G. Brennan in Special Narcotics courts. The entire ride downtown I just kept thinking how the fuck these niggas knew where I lived at; I never use my wife address for nothing. Once we got to central bookings I asked one of the detectives that transported us downtown; how did ya'll know where to find me?

He stated: he rode on the elevator with me twice, and watched to see what floor I got off on. (WOW)

Bigg Bill and I both were charged with Criminal Sales of a Controlled Substance 3rd 220.39 and Criminal Sales of a Controlled Substance 2nd 220.41. Them 220.39 charges all those were B felonies but them 220.41 charges were A-2.

Section 220.39 Criminal sale of a controlled substance in the third degree

A person is guilty of criminal sale of a controlled substance in the third degree when he knowingly and unlawfully sells:

1. A narcotic drug; or

2. A stimulant, hallucinogen, hallucinogenic substance, or lysergic acid diethylamide and has previously been convicted of an offense defined in article two hundred twenty or the attempt or conspiracy to commit any such offense; or

3. A stimulant and the stimulant weighs one gram or more; or

4. Lysergic acid diethylamide and the lysergic acid diethylamide weighs one milligram or more; or

5. A hallucinogen and the hallucinogen weighs twenty-five milligrams or more; or

6. A hallucinogenic substance and the hallucinogenic substance weighs one gram or more; or

7. One or more preparations, compounds, mixtures or substances containing methamphetamine, its salts, isomers or salts of isomers and the preparations, compounds, mixtures or substances are of an aggregate weight of one-eighth ounce or more; or

8. Phencyclidine and the phencyclidine weighs two hundred fifty milligrams or more; or

9. A narcotic preparation to a person less than twenty-one years old.

Criminal sale of a controlled substance in the third degree is a class B felony.

Section 220.41 Criminal sale of a controlled substance in the second degree

A person is guilty of criminal sale of a controlled substance in the second degree when he knowingly and unlawfully sells:

1. One or more preparations, compounds, mixtures or substances containing a narcotic drug and the preparations, compounds, mixtures or substances are of an aggregate weight of one-half ounce or more; or

2. One or more preparations, compounds, mixtures or substances containing methamphetamine, its salts, isomers or salts of isomers and the preparations, compounds, mixtures or substances are of an aggregate weight of one-half ounce or more; or

3. A stimulant and the stimulant weighs five grams or more; or

4. Lysergic acid diethylamide and the lysergic acid diethylamide weighs five milligrams or more; or

5. A hallucinogen and the hallucinogen weighs one hundred twenty-five milligrams or more; or

6. A hallucinogenic substance and the hallucinogenic substance weighs five grams or more; or

7. Methadone and the methadone weigh three hundred sixty milligrams or more.

Criminal sale of a controlled substance in the second degree is a class A-II felony.

	NON-VIOLENT PREDICATE NON-VIOLENT (PENAL LAW 70.06)		NON-VIOLET PREDICATE VIOLENT (PENAL LAW 70.06)	
	MIN.	MAX.	MIN.	MAX.
A-2	6 - 12 1/2	LIFE		
B	4 1/2 - 9	12 1/2 - 25	8	25
C	3 - 6	7 1/2 - 15	5	15
D	2 - 4	3 1/2 - 7	3	7
E	1 1/2 - 3	2 - 4	2	4

If the defendant has a PRIOR NON-VIOLENT felony conviction, he will be sentenced as a "second felony offender." For a non-violent second felony, sentences are indeterminate. If the second offense is violent, the sentence will be determinate.

Just off the 220.41 charges alone I was facing 6 – 12 years if I go to trial, shit was about to get ugly. At arraignment I waved my right to a Grand Jury Hearing and the Assistant District Attorney (ADA) asked for a "72 hour surety bail", which was granted by the Judge and set at $50,000 bond over $20,000 cash. A surety bail was just a bail hearing meaning that the ADA is concerned that the defendant might be able to have his bail posted, or any bail bond posted by illicit funds (Drug Money). I was sent over to Manhattan Detention Complex (MDC) on 125 White Street. The Manhattan Detention Complex consists of two buildings designated the North and South Towers, connected by a bridge. The North Tower was opened in 1990. The South Tower, formerly the Manhattan House of Detention, or the "Tombs," was opened in 1983, after a complete remodeling. The complex houses male detainees, most of them undergoing the intake process or facing trial in New York County (Manhattan).

I was due to appear back in court on the 8th of May, which was in 5 days I needed a care package. After being process for over 15 hours I was finally assigned to a housing unit on Friday, a little after 12pm. As soon as I reached my housing unit 10 minutes later I was being called for a visit. My brother Melvin Sleepz & Topboss came to check me and brought me some clothes and a few books. I just pulled up and I was already on it. I knew I was getting a bail so I had wifey already on her shit. MDC houses only male inmates, most of them pretrial detainees. The combined capacity of the two buildings is about 900 people. I was placed in the South Tower, 8 West. If I can recall this was the same house I was in, back in 1995, when I got booked in the Port Authority. I was ready to get comfortable, I had my books, sweat suits and money on the books, but Cassy on the other hand she wasn't with me getting all comfortable in shit, so the very next morning she posted my $20,000 cash bail.

Since I had a 72-hour Surety the Assistant District Attorney had to sign off on it, she have 72 hours from the posting of the bail/bond to investigate the funds and then to either have a hearing on the issue, or consent of my release. My bail was posted Saturday morning so I still had to wait to be brought back to court on Monday. Unfortunately that's the way it works, Corrections has to produce me in Court everyday once the bail is posted. My initial Court day, which is also my 180.80-day, was on Tuesday but if the Assistant District Attorney Sandra Talbott approves my bail, I'll walk right out the courthouse. After giving my wife the run around for 2 days straight, the fucking A.D.A still denied my bail. She wanted to know where there money came from, and who money was it; my wife had to bring pay-stubs, tax returns, bank statements, all kind of Identification just to prove that the money was legit and my bail was still denied. The way shit was looking, the only way I'll be walking out those gates is when I get a date for parole, it was really time to get comfortable.

CHAPTER 26

After being indicted my next court date was adjourn to June 5th over in Supreme Court in 111 Centre Street Part 22. I was sent back to MDC for the next 2 weeks before being transferred over to Riker's Island, NYC main jail complex. Riker's Island is located out in East Elmhurst Queens. I was placed in GMDC (George Motchan Detention Center) also known as C-73 or the 3 Building. I didn't know what to expect, I have never been on Riker's Island up until today but I did know this I wasn't going home anytime soon so I was not going for none of the sucker shit. This might have been my first time on Riker's but this wasn't my first rodeo, I knew how to jail. The violence on Riker's was out of control it didn't matter what building you went too, it was the niggas in the building that made it wild, you didn't only have to worry about the inmate's getting at you if you was the Fake Tough type, you had to watch out for them C.O's too they was on their bullshit washing niggas up.

The morning I was due to appear in court Judge Robert Stolz was on the bench as the A.D.A read of my indictment:

SUPREME COURT OF THE STATE OF NEW YORK
COUNTY OF NEW YORK
SPECIAL NARCOTICS PARTS

THE PEOPLE OF THE STATE OF NEW YORK

- Against -

TROY HOUGH

Defendant

CRIMINAL SALE OF A CONTROLLED SUBSTANCE IN THE SECOND DEGREE (HOUGH – 2 COUNTS)

CRIMINAL SALE OF A CONTROLLED SUBSTANCE IN THE THIRD DEGREE (HOUGH – 7 COUNTS)

DOCKET NO.
2012NY034995

The people intend to prove that defendant Troy Hough, acted as principal and/ or an accomplice in the commission of the crimes charged in that on December 7, 2011; December 9, 2011; December 16, 2011; December 21, 2011; December 30, 2011; and January 4, 2012 the defendant acted in concert to sell a narcotic drug, to wit, cocaine, to an undercover police officer. On January 12, 2012; January 26, 2012; and February 11, 2012, defendant Troy Hough sold a narcotic drug, to wit, cocaine, to an undercover police officer, and on January 26, 2012 and February 11, 2012, said cocaine weighed in excess of ½ of an ounce.

E. **RECIPROCAL DISCOVERY**
Pursuant to CPL §240.30(1), the People hereby demand that defendant supply the District Attorney with (a) any written report or document, or portion thereof, concerning a physical or mental examination, or scientific test, experiment, or comparisons, made by or at the request or direction of the defendant, if the defendant intends to introduce such report or document at trial, or if defendant has filed a notice of intent to proffer psychiatric evidence and such report or document which relates thereto or if such report or document was made by a person other than defendant, whom defendant intends to call as a witness at trial; and (b) any photograph, drawing, tape, or other electronic recording which the defendant intends to introduce at trial.

F. **ADDITIONAL DISCLOSURES**
On December 21, 2011, UC 202, through a photographic array, misidentified an individual as the person later learned to be Troy Hough. Between February 3, 2012 and February 9, 2012, UC 202 determined that Troy Hough, and not the first individual, was, in fact, the person selling drugs to UC 202.

NOTE: Any defense motion or request addressed to the above-captioned indictment should be directed to the attention of the Assistant District Attorney named below, who is assigned to this case

DATED: New York, New York
May 25, 2012

Respectfully submitted,

Bridget G. Brennan
Special Narcotics Prosecutor
80 Centre Street
New York, New York 10013

Sandra Talbott
Sandra Talbott
Assistant District Attorney

Some people say it's loophole in every case so of course I'm looking through my paperwork for any fuck ups. They had me red handed on every sell I made to Dez, every date, location, and Laboratory report was accurate, up until I read my <u>Additional Disclosures</u> where the UC 202 misidentified me in a photographic array. The undercover identified me as a person name Gregory Hooks several different times before realizing that Troy Hough and not the first individual, was in fact, the person selling drugs to the UC 202. The case was put on the calendar for a later date on the 23rd of July but I made a mental note of it and had my lawyer come visit me on the Island so we could discuss it over.

Visiting a loved one on Riker's Island is one hell of a process; you almost have to block out a whole day just for an hour visit. First stop is the registration building, where the lines to get in are long even at 7am on morning visits. After an ID check, you'll eventually pass through airport-like security and X-rays, get questioned, fill out some forms, then you wait to get shuttled to the actual detention facility. After another long wait comes another round of metal-detectors and X-ray machines. Then comes another security check in a private vestibule where you have to lift your tongue and fold down your waistband to prove you're not bringing stuff in. Then it's another wait of about an hour before the actual visit. I told Cassy just come visit me twice a month and I was good, I didn't want her going through all that we talked on the phone everyday anyway unless the building was on lockdown.

The 3 building was Litt, a lot of niggas got taken off the count tho, every other day somebody was getting shot, (***stabbed or cut***) or niggas was popping that bottle, (***fighting***) that red alarm stayed ringing off but other then that C-73 was sweet as hell, it was always Tobacco and Bud in the building even Alcohol. One thing I hate to do in jail is just lay around and do nothing that's not me I have to have some type of movement through out the building, so I got myself a job working in the storehouse / laundry room. I had to keep busy I knew I was going to be here for a while. From 5am – 1pm Monday - Friday I was never in my housing unit. I didn't get a job for the money, my wife made sure the balance in my inmate account never hit $0.00 and that's a fact, I did it for the movement, but it helped.

Now a day with this new technology, social media makes it much easier for family and friends to stay connected with loved one's that's incarcerated as well as providing for them across the country. It's websites that's been created where you are able to send money to friends or family members that's incarcerated from the privacy of your own home within minutes. It's the fastest and most secure way to send money and it's more convenient. My wife used to always use **Jpay.com**. JPay is the most trusted name in corrections they offer their customer service to over 30 states across the country.

CHAPTER 27

      Like a week or so before I was due to return to court on the 23rd of July my Lawyer came through and paid me a Legal Visit. We sat there for over an hour going over the case and my paperwork. I had a few loopholes I might be able to use as leverage but it wasn't enough to beat all 9 counts, I needed the fucking ADA to come off that 6-year offer. They had video evidence of me on various sells and to make things worst the Special Assistance District Attorney of the Special Narcotics Courts, Bridget G. Brennan was charging me as a Predicate. A predicate is a Second felony offenders – or people with predicate felony convictions being sentenced on a new felony – are most commonly classified as either second violent felony offenders, regular (non-violent) felony offenders, or second felony drug offenders. I was charged as a Second Felony Drug Offender. This was my first felony in NYC since 1995 when I copped out to 5 years probation, how was that possible I asked; My lawyer said they was using my Connecticut conviction against me and it's only been 9½ years since then not 10. That conviction was in another state but the same jurisdiction. The ADA was playing hardball with me, first she denied my bail, now she pushing for a predicate conviction (smh). Going Upstate wasn't even a question I knew I was going up but for how long, is what I really wanted to know.

As long as you have money in your account you're allowed to make a 21 minute phone call to any number you choose to dial, once every 5 hours but if you don't have any money corrections will allow you to make one 6 minute local phone call once a day and on Sunday's you are giving 4 free 6 minute calls if your balance in your account is $0.00. The 6 min phone calls isn't free, it's credited to your account and as soon as you receive money every 6-minute phone call you made, is deducted from your account. Some niggas didn't care they knew nobody wasn't sending them a dime so they sold their 6 min calls everyday. I had a few niggas on contracts by the week, I paid niggas in advance so I'll use them extra 6 min slots to holla at my niggas in the town. Beside hollering at my lil bro Melvin Sleepz and Topboss, I use to stay calling my nigga R.G phone to see what was shaking in the hood. R.G was one of my niggas that grew up in the hood too trying to find a way out and just like me R.G found his self in trouble with the law and had to take a few vacations as well. R.G was well familiar with the Island and how the phone system worked so every time he seen that **(718) 777 - 4360** number pop up he was on point, because once you let the answering machine pick up, that's 67 cent, gone out of your account, and your 6 min call is dead. My weekly phone bill was like $30 - $40.

I had a little routine going on for myself that kept me busy on a daily basic, besides working I stayed at the poker table gambling my money and I also read a lot. I had about 70 hood novels total by the time I left Riker's Island, Cassy use to send me 4 books dam near every week. Every night anytime between 7-8pm unless we were on lockdown I was on the phone that was my slot, no later then 8:30 I was cooking my dinner getting ready to call it a night. I was in a 50 man dorm so it wasn't all that peaceful in there only time it got quiet is when the lights went out and most of the time that didn't even work. We had a few of them " Yo I'm trying sleep ass niggas " or " ya'll making too much noise " living amongst us, so my favorite response to them niggas was;

"BailOut or PackUp" You wasn't sleeping in New York!

Pretty much nothing happened on the 23rd when I went back to court, just the ADA, my Lawyer and the Judge talking, back and forth about a bunch of Mumbo – Jumbo, again my case was adjourned and placed on the calendar for the 10th of September and this time they were ready. That was 7 weeks away, 49 days to be exact but that shit came around so fast, because before I knew it, I was back in them bullpens waiting to go to court. The pens were pack; it was a lot of buses leaving from GMDC that morning. Manhattan criminal courts had 4 buses going out not including the buses for 111 courts and for the Bronx's, it was a lot going on. All 4 buses for Manhattan courts and the 2 buses for the Bronx's, pulled up already usually 111 courts be the first to go but not today I didn't get to court until 11am.

NoMoreStateGreens

CHAPTER 28

As soon as I reached the pens my lawyer came to get me. I was taken to a small visiting area where my lawyer and I can talk before we went out in front of the judge. Once I sat down she let me know that my case was put over until the 23rd of October but they also made me an offer more like a;

"Take it or Leave it offer"

The ADA offered me 4 years with 3 years Post-Release Supervision.

" 4 years sheesh, with 3 years post " I thought but at least they took the 6 years off the table.

My lawyer also mention the ADA was charging as a predicate but since this was my first state bid in NYC I was eligible for the Shock Incarceration Program; she was going to ask the judge if I can be mandated to a shock facility. I had 43 days to think it over but I didn't need 43 days my mind was set I was jumping on those 4 years fuck that. I told my lawyer I'll take the 4 years but try and see if you can get me 3 years instead. Shock is a six-month program that is similar in nature to a military boot camp regimen, but it incorporates intensive substance abuse treatment and academic education within a therapeutic community setting. Sentenced offenders can enter the Shock Incarceration program if they are legally eligible, if the Department of Correctional Services (DOCS) staff determines they are suitable for the program. To qualify, offenders must be under 50 and eligible for parole within 3 years of admission to DOCS. They must not have committed a violent or sexual offense or been previously sentenced to an indeterminate prison term. By the looks of it I was most definitely eligible so I should qualify, that 6-month program sounded way better then that 4 years. I heard all the stories about shock how them Drill instructors be yelling all in your face humiliating you, I didn't care tho I was just going to have to deal with it.

     I been on Riker's Island for 6 months and I was ready to go, I knew I wasn't going home I just wanted to get this time started and over with. It was that time again but today was different I knew what was about to go down. I pleaded down to a B felony and copped out to 4 years with 3 years Post-Release Supervision for Criminal Sells of Controlled Substance 3rd. I also took my plea as a Second Felony Drug Offender.

SPECIAL NARCOTICS COURTS
SUPREME COURT OF THE STATE OF NEW YORK
CITY OF NEW YORK

THE PEOPLE OF THE STATE OF NEW YORK,

— against —

TROY HOUGH,

Defendant.

STATEMENT OF PREDICATE FELONY CONVICTION PURSUANT TO CRIMINAL PROCEDURE LAW §400.21 AND PENAL LAW §70.70, RELATIVE TO INDICTMENT NUMBER: 2038/2012

I, BRIDGET G. BRENNAN, Special Assistant District Attorney of the Special Narcotics Courts, do hereby allege, pursuant to C.P.L. §400.21, that the above-named defendant has previously been subjected to a predicate felony conviction as defined in P.L. §70.06, and is a Second Felony Drug Offender as defined in P.L. §70.70. The defendant's predicate felony conviction is described below:

On March 17, 1998, in the Superior Court of Hartford County in the State of Connecticut, the defendant was convicted of the offense of Possession of Narcotics with Intent to Sell, Conn. Gen. Stat. § 21a 277(a), an offense for which a sentence to a term of imprisonment in excess of one year or a sentence of death was authorized in that jurisdiction and is authorized in this state.

The ten-year period referred to in Penal Law §70.06(1)(b)(v) is extended by defendant's incarceration at the Connecticut Department of Corrections from October 10, 1996 to November 8, 1996; August 7, 1997 and July 7, 2000; December 11, 2001 and January 31, 2003.

DATED: New York, New York
October 22, 2012

BRIDGET G. BRENNAN
Special Assistant District Attorney
Special Narcotics Court

BY: _____
Assistant District Attorney

I was due to return back to court on the 5th of November for sentencing but before I get sentence I have to do a Pre-Sentence Investigation (PSI). A Pre-sentence Investigation is a legal term referring to the investigation into the history of person convicted of a crime before sentencing to determine if there are extenuating circumstances, which should ameliorate the sentence or a history of criminal behavior to increase the harshness of the sentence. Due to the super storm Hurricane Sandy that flooded most of the city Manhattan courts were shut down which lead me to being sentence a month later on December 12th 2012. After I was sentence I was transferred over to ARDC - C-74 I was now officially state ready.

CHAPTER 29

Here we go again I was about to miss another birthday, another Christmas, another New Years and every one of my son's birthday's shit, it felt like déjà vu. Once again because of my poor decision-making I'm a statistic to the Department Of Corrections. I was transferred to Ulster Correctional/Reception Facility upstate in Napanoch, NY (Ulster County) 90 miles north of the city where I received 3 sets of my own personal pair of State Greens. As soon as we enter the facility them Red Necks let it be known;

"You are no longer on Riker's Island" So act up if you want!

This was one of the first spot besides Downstate Correctional Facility and Elmira Correctional; you have to make after being sentence in New York and turned over to the State, these White boys were not trying to play with you straight hands & feet, welcome to Ulster County. I was the 3,768 person in 2012 to be giving a pair of State Greens in Ulster and it was still 11 days left before the year ended. In 2012, alone the Department of Corrections gave out 13,551 x 3 = 40,653 pair of State Greens and that's not including all the Parole Violators that's a lot of pair of State Greens. Downstate had

5,768 new inmates in 2012 come through their reception, Elmira had 3,922 new inmates and Ulster had 3,861. In the department of corrections eyes, I was no longer a person I was just a number to them, 12R3768 and I will remain that number until 8/15/2016.

Ulster reminded me of Enfield CI, the way all of the buildings were connected by paved roadways. The entire facility was surrounded by an exterior 17- foot fence and an eight-foot interior fence, both covered and wrapped with razor ribbons, it's no getting over that. All new state inmates start a five-day schedule of reception/classification activities upon arrival. The purpose of this process is to determine an inmate's classification and placement collect information for the destination facility. Returned parole violators are put through a similar classification process, which is accomplished in just three days. Establishing an inmate's placement consists of determining his security classification as well as his program, medical and mental health needs. A Correction Counselor determines an inmate's security classification. An inmate's medical needs are determined after a complete physical and dental exam, which includes diagnostic X-rays and lab work. The Office of Mental Hygiene (OMH) provides a psychologist at Ulster to identify programs for those inmates identified as having mental health needs. The typical stay at Ulster is approximately 30 days or more. The Department Of Corrections has 59 correctional facilities that's open as of today with 4 of them being for women.

Now Riker's Island was already crazy I had to deal with niggas from all parts of the city it was 5 different boroughs on that island, but now it get a little more serious it's nigga's from different County's from all parts of New York State up in here I had to really be on point. After I finish with my assessment it was just a waiting game. The nature of the crime was non-violent so I was already eligible for the Shock Program but first I had to be medically approved. I spent my 22nd, 23rd, 24th, 26th, 27th, birthday in prison and now I spending my 37th birthday up in Ulster County. It really didn't bother me what bother me was, the fact that it didn't bother me at all, I just think I've gotten numb to it. When I first got to Ulster I had the waves spinning but not now (Pa-Pa) I had the fresh clean baldy with the rapist face. It was freezing up there but that wasn't shit, that was just the beginning it's about to get colder further upstate. I wasn't allowed to receive a package up until 30 days but as soon as I was allowed I immediately had one sent up. I needed some Thermals, a Skully Hat, some Tobacco and food. I was able to shake a move for the New Years one of my niggas from the BX I came up from the island with had his shorty come through I had my brother Melvin Sleepz met up with her and drop some Tobacco off before she came up. Ulster was 1 big transportation hub from Monday – Friday inmates was coming and going. Once you are convicted of a crime in New York State it's mandatory that you pay a surcharge fee, or fine of $375.00 unless the Commitment States: "Waived by the Courts", "Not to be Paid until after Release", Do Not Collect by Civil Judgment", "Not to be Deducted from Prison Account", or Not to be Collected by DOCCS while incarcerated. If you have none of the above then you must pay before you can receive any funds to your account. My surcharge was paid immediately I couldn't afford to be missing commissary. Out the $375 dollars $300 of that was a Mandatory Surcharge, for what I don't know, $25 went towards (CVAF) Crime Victim Assistance Fee's and the $50 was for my DNA. I was lucky enough just to have 1 surcharge few niggas I ran into had 2 & 3 surcharges.

 I stayed at Ulster for 7 weeks when my day finally came and I was on the Draft.

CHAPTER 30

I was approved to go to Shock so I was transferred to Lakeview Shock C. F. further upstate in Brocton NY. Being handcuffed is a horrible and sometimes painful experience. The worst for me was being shackled/handcuffed to a waist chain and leg irons-for 10 hours. Imagine traveling in a bus with bars on the window, shackles around your waist with handcuffs attached, and leg irons with cuffs around your ankles. You can feel the metal cutting against the flesh of your wrists and ankles, such that when the cuffs are removed there are red rings around your wrists. The Department Of Corrections has a few rules when being transported and that is "No Talking" while the bus is in motion, only when we stop. "No Shitting " in the toilet, so watch what you eat and when the bus stops it's no getting up out of your seat not even to use the bathroom. We were about 36 deep on that bus but only 20 of us were going to Lakeview, the rest were getting dropped off at Gowanda, & Collins Correctional Facility. It was a different type of cold up there in Lakeview, we was about 50 miles south of Buffalo in far western New York, about a quarter-mile from the Lake Erie shore and an hour away from outside of Ohio.

Shock is a correctional program with a military theme. Beds must be made just so and lockers maintained exactly as prescribed. Inmates must be properly shaved and attired at all times. Inmates wishing to speak to staff must ask permission, and must begin and end every utterance with "sir" or "ma'am." Inattention, carelessness, tardiness, sloth, "attitude" and other departures from expectations are corrected on the spot with "learning experiences," such as moving a rock pile, dropping for eight-count pushups or carrying a log around all day. The military component is not the toughest part of shock. For six months, most inmates can handle getting yelled at and all the physical training but when it comes to the treatment that's the tough part about Shock.

Lakeview had a well-known reputation putting hands and feet's on you, as soon as we got off the bus I didn't only witness it, I was also a victim. This 1 Female C/O smacked flames out of me for lining up wrong. When they say keep your eye's and your ears open and your mouth shut they really mean that shit. It was freezing cold that night when we pulled up, the temperature was 21 degree's with an 8-degree wind-chill and it was snowing. You are not allowed to wear any headgear material during transit when being transferred from facility to facility so I didn't have a hat on when that funky bitch smack me in my head. All I thought to myself was, this was going to be a long ass 180 days. For 1 it's to cold for this shit, smacking me in my mother fucken head like that, and for 2, I been on that bus for 10 hours, I was starving and tired I wasn't paying attention. Shit went from 0 – 100 real quick with this military shit I signed up for they didn't waste anytime they got straight down to business. Whatever I didn't know about this program I was about to find out. Everything was in military terms;

      Bathrooms were called: The Head
      Beds were called: Racks

I had to ask for permission to speak and permission to be dismissed. We couldn't use the word I we had to refer to ourselves as This Inmate.
Example:

Inmate: Sir Permission to speak Sir

Drill Instructor: Speak

Inmate: Sir this inmate would like to borrow the needle and thread Sir

Drill Instructor: Here you go

Inmate: Sir permission to be dismissed Sir

Drill Instructor: Dismissed

Inmate: Sir Yes Sir

I was already told at the sound of a whistle blowing early in the morning I was too hop up out of my rack yelling and screaming and to stand at the Position of Attention. We had to stand up straight and pull our shoulders back so they don't slouch, put the heels of both feet together, and point our toes out roughly 45 degrees from the center so your feet form a V shape. Ball our fists, but not too tight, and hold our arms at our sides keeping our elbows slightly bent with our Face forward keeping our chin level with the floor, focusing straight ahead. After that we had 8 minutes to get Dress, Shave, Wash our Face & Brush our Teeth plus make up our Racks we slept in (Military Style) 4 corners and this same procedure was going to last for 180 days. My 180 days don't officially start until I get into a Platoon none of this shit was counting.

    After being in Lakeview for 2 weeks I was transferred to Moriah Shock Incarceration Correctional Facility in Mineville N.Y near Port Henry in the Adirondack Mountains on Valentine's Day with the 2nd Platoon. February 14th was day 1 of my 180 days I was officially now in a platoon. The 2nd Platoon was also known as THE MIGHTY WOLFPACKS, THE DEUCE, or (2.46). Moriah was way better then Lakeview, It was a lot smaller, but it was way closer to the city then Lakeview was. Moriah only had 6 Platoons where as Lakeview had about 10. The Drill Instructors in Moriah were no different tho they were just older in age. As soon as we got off the bus we were told to grab the first draft bag we saw and "double time it" (RUN) into the gymnasium.

For the first 2 weeks which is called zero weeks is one of the hardest parts of the program but if you can make it through zero weeks then the next 26 weeks shouldn't be about nothing. We must learn the basics of physical training, drill and ceremony, and discipline. It's like orientation, indoctrination, and initial evaluation with a focus on strict discipline and attention to detail. Most dropouts occur during zero weeks niggas can't handle it or just don't want to. The way I was feeling it wasn't about me anymore, it was about getting home to my wife and kids. I haven't seen my wife since December right before I left Rikers Island but we spoke on the phone everyday while I was up in Ulster but all that shit came to an end once I was transferred. I was only able to call home every other week for 10 minutes only, now that was stressful. Every morning from 5:45 to 6:30 we had to perform calisthenics and from 6:30 to 7:15 complete a 3 - 5 mile run. They had us marching to and from all activities in platoon or squad formation on some real army shit.

Daily Schedule for Offenders in New York Shock Incarceration Facilities

```
5:25 Wake up and standing count
5:45 6:30 Calisthenics and drill
6:30-7:15 Run 3 — 5 miles
7:15-8:00 Mandatory breakfast/cleanup
8:15 Standing count and company formation
8:30-11:55 Work/school schedules
12:00-12:30 Mandatory lunch and standing count
12:30-2:30 Afternoon work/school schedule
2:30-4:00 3 minute Showers
4:00-4:45 Network community meeting
4:45-5:45 Mandatory dinner, prepare for evening
6:00-9:00 School, group counseling, drug
Counseling, prerelease counseling, decision making
classes
8:00 count while in programs
9:15-9:30 Squad bay cleanup, prepare for bed
9:30 Standing count, lights out
```

To make it through this program you not only had to make it through the physical part; failing Daily and Weekly Evaluations can also get you kicked out of the program so you had to pass those. We were evaluated on the way our boots shined, if the creases in our state greens were sharp enough, or if we shaved well enough, it was crazy and a lot of niggas couldn't get that right. It was a few that never ironed their own clothes in their life or even uses an iron at all. Your boots had to be looking like glass slippers if you couldn't see a reflection they weren't shined good enough, wordjo! I'm not going to even hold you, but I was like one of the top 5 that had the best looking boots in the Deuce. We also were graded on our bunks and our lockers and it's contents, our bunks had to be perfect (a certain measurement in the fold of the sheets) and for the lockers kept dust free.

The 2nd Platoon was run by D.I Roc and D.I Magee, but the overall commander and chief of this facility was Superintendent B. McCormick and his underboss Captain Rawson. These 2 played no games, Superintendent McCormick use to check our fingernails making sure they were cut and clean, Captain Rawson use to always G-check us on our General Orders. Man-O-Man I feel for you if you got caught with long or dirty nails or didn't know any 1 of your general orders. When we arrived at Shock we was giving a S.M.A.R.T. Book and we had to memorize it plus carry with us at all times, don't get caught without it (smh). Captain Rawson was also big on shoestrings he hated to see them hanging out of your sneakers, we had to keep them tucked in or the whole platoon was going to pay for it.

D.I Roc was our A – Officer he was a beast and nothing to play with. This old nigga had to be in his 50's and his workout game was crazy. He had us doing 1500 – 2500 Side Straddle Hops (jumping jacks) and then run 5 miles right after that. We were the only Platoon running 5 miles regardless of weather everyday from Sunday – Wednesday. One thing I really respected about D.I Roc was he never embarrassed us in front of the other platoons he kept The Deuce business inside the Deuce. Now D.I Magee he didn't give a fuck, he would embarrass us anywhere, one time niggas was arguing during the run that nigga stop us right in the middle of the road and made us get in a Front Leaning Rest Position, for like 10 mins, he hated noise we couldn't talk at all when he was on shift it was straight Quiet Time. D.I Magee was straight up tho, Miserable as fuck but straight up. It was a few things I liked about D.I Magee for 1 he gave us wild smoke breaks and for 2 he gave us open showers, where as he let us run them, we wasn't on the time clock but we all had to be dress by 3:25pm. He uses to let us start the showers at 2:30pm that was almost an hour we had. It was 37 of us total, and 6 showers. D.I Roc ran the showers Sunday-Wednesday he started the clock at 2:55 and gave us 3 minutes apiece we had to go in there 6 at a time (No Homo). Other then that D.I Magee gave us hell especially once we became Top Dogs and received our Gold Caps.

It's 3 stages you must go through when you get there it shows progress within the program. We started off wearing Green Caps for the first 10 weeks, then we switch to the Red Caps for the next 8 weeks then finally we receive our Gold Caps and became Top Dogs until Graduation Day. The 2nd Platoon was schedule to graduate on 8-15-2013, we got there 2-14-2013. Some people might look at it and be like that 6 months, 26 weeks, 180 days or however you want to put it isn't shit, but in reality if you never went through it you wouldn't know. It's really a mental thing you have to bite your tongue for everything, especially once you get halfway through the program you don't want to get kicked out after all that time, but that's when all the soft niggas start talking shit getting tough. They know you not going to punch they face off in there but I bet you if we were in another spot that same nigga would be a church mouse. I witness niggas have 5 months in actually 28 days left to graduate, fuck up and get sent to Comstock Correctional for some dum shit. You had to be a real (Shit Bird) to get kicked out the program with less then 30 days left to go home. You really have to learn how to control your temper and don't let your emotions get the best of you if you want to make it through the program. Believe me I was tested everyday I lost my cool a few times that could have cost me my program, luckily my fellow inmates wasn't ready to lose their program. Nigga's used to do wild sucker shit and don't "man up" to it, and that shit use to have me tight. Once a person don't Man Up to it the whole platoon got to pay for it. They were good for making the whole platoon pay for 1 person fuck up. Like this one time Captain Rawson came to our Platoon and caught 1 person with his shoestrings hanging out of his sneakers, he made the whole platoon line up outside in our socks with our sneakers in our hand and made us toss them down this steep ass hill all at once. 37 x 2 = That's 74 pair of New Balance's went flying down the hill, then he made us go get them & we was timed on that. Yo niggas was grabbing 2 left feet's, different sizes it didn't matter we had to hurry up next time he might make up throw our clothes. They were good for that shit blowing up locker's throwing everybody shit together in one pile. They told us when we got there to tag everything T-shirts, boxers, socks, gloves, hat's, cosmetics everything so when an explosion happen your shit not hard to find.

CHAPTER 31

      6 months is really not a long time especially to a person that done time before but everybody knows that once you get to 90 days or less it get harder because now you start counting down the days you have left to go home. My wife and I had a nice little set up going on between us she visited me once a month and wrote me letters once a week. Saturdays and Sundays was the only free time we had to ourselves so on those days, I use my time to write letters home. Every other week I was able to call home but only for 10 mins I hated that shit but I had to deal with it, it was almost over tho. One of my Visits Days fell on Mother's Day, I wasn't to sure if my wife was still going to show or not but she did, I really respected her for that, she wasn't being selfish and just thinking about herself she took time out on her day to ride up on a van for 6 hours to sit in a visiting room. This was her 3rd visit we had 3 more to go and it will be allover that's how I counted my days downs. It felt like the time just slowed up all of sudden all I was thinking about was going home in 2 more months, but the time was dragging by slow I needed something to do. I always wanted to write

a book but I didn't know what kind of book I wanted to write Fiction or Non-fiction then I thought, an Autobiography of my life would be the easiest I didn't have to make shit up. It was certain information I needed that I didn't have or knew at the time so I had to wait until I went home to do research on.

D.I Roc was due to go on vacation and wasn't due to return until September after we graduated. Every platoon before they graduate must complete a Captains Run (run the most miles you can run), and to my knowledge or what I've been told that the 2nd platoon holds that reputation in running the most miles. D.I Roc like I said earlier is a beast every month he runs in a Captains Run with the other platoons and he try to make them niggas run 10 miles but they can't hang. The whole 6 months them niggas was running 1-2 miles a day sometimes 3 but not us, everyday we ran 5 miles with D.I Roc sometime 6 miles. He was preparing us early he even made us do our Captains run 1½ month early. Captains Runs are schedule to be ran 4 days before graduation not a month in a half earlier but guess what since he was going on vacation that schedule changed. We ran 12 miles that morning all 37 of us "The Mighty Mighty Wolfpack" we ran 12 miles in 2 hours non-stop S/o to platoon 2.46 (Hoorah). For the whole 6 months we ran a total of 440 miles and I lost about 15 pounds.

D.I Magee was our full time officer now and man he gave us hell, he didn't like to run as much maybe 2 miles a day with him. D.I Magee gave us a lot of rec time tho and put a few of us on work crews to work down in Albany. Working in Albany was one of the best work assignments ever we was in the hoods. For 9 hours Monday thru Thursday we were off the compound, site seeing. Once we became Top Dogs the pressure was on us we had to lead by example.

      August 15, 2013 finally came, Graduation Day and in a few more hours I'll be going home. Graduation ceremonies are attended by DOCS officials and State dignitaries, often including judges, the Governor, and State legislators, in addition to family members and friends. Graduation certificates are presented, and special awards are made to the two inmates with the highest and the most improved evaluation scores. I didn't care about getting any awards I just wanted to go home. I completed the program successfully but I still wasn't done my next task was to complete the 3 years of Post Supervision Parole I had on the back of my sentence. I was due to report to the Bronx 1 Area Office, on 82 Lincoln Ave in the Bronx to Parole Officer M. Cartagena at 8:30am 24 hours of my release.

NoMoreStateGreens

Epilogue

Being on parole was a scary feeling for me the last thing I wanted to happen was to go back up north on a Violation for having Police contact. I wasn't too worried about violating curfew or dirty urines because I was playing by the rules. I didn't have to go to none of them Drug outpatient Programs or nor did my P.O sweat me about having a job. The Job part she didn't have too sweat me about I was already on it. Being on parole kind of help me change my life into the direction I'm going now and hopefully remain there. While on parole I was introduce to this program called CEO "Center Employment Opportunities". The Center for Employment Opportunities (CEO) program is dedicated to providing immediate, effective and comprehensive employment services to men and women with recent criminal convictions. I was able to obtain my 10-hour Osha Certification along with my Carpentry and Plumbing Certificates. No More State Greens is definitely my model and what I stand by. I'm not saying I'm never going back because who knows what can happen, but I will say this I don't ever want too. I consider myself one of the lucky one's that got another chance at life, I was sentence to 4 years and out the 4 years I did 15½ months total and was back home. 7½ months on Riker's Island, 2 months in Ulster and 6 months in Moriah Shock. I'm currently off parole as of today, which I was scheduled to be release 8-15-2016. I was discharge on 8-15-2014, 2 years earlier for good behavior I guess, I just thank god for everything maybe I needed to go back to jail so I can really see if this is the life I wanted to be in. My worst fear is me spending the rest of my life in somebody prison cell especially for something I'll regret doing after the fact. I washed my hands; I'm done with the Drug Game I just want to live life comfortable not worrying if the Feds going to come get me next. I still continue to make music, and I also started my own painting company with my brother Melvin Sleepz "BloodBrothersPaintingLLC".

NO MORE STATE GREENS
THE TRILOGY

???????

Let's Hope Not

Don't miss the thrilling beginning of
K-Lou new series!!!!!!

Please turn this page for a
Preview of

PRIDE OF A HUSTLER

Chapter 1

On March 18, 2000, the prison gates of Carl Robinson opened to free Jaquan Johnson, after serving a five-year bid for five counts of possession of narcotics. Jaquan was a ruthless dude in his community. He was well known for his brutal attacks on other hustlers. Jaquan was six foot, two- hundred and thirty pounds and all muscle; which was very intimidating to others. He sported a low cut with waves and a gold T for his baby face look. Jaquan now 24 years old with no kids, and was finally free. He had no one monitoring his movements.

After waiting an hour to be cut loose into his high school girlfriend's arms, he felt happy again. As his girlfriend Sheena yelled to the top of her lungs with tears flowing down her face, "Look at my baby, Oh my God look at my baby." She hugged and kissed him like she just won a million bucks. Sheena's been waiting for this day since he first got sentenced in New Britain back in 1995.

"Damn baby you look good, so sexy I just wanna get to business right now." Jaquan smiled at his long time loving girlfriend and said "let's get out of here; I don't ever wanna see these prisons again." With that thought Sheena jumped into her Caravan and they drove away.

Once on the highway back to New Britain, Jaquan looked out his window seeing how much things have changed. He rolled down his window to feel the fresh air and said, "Damn bae everything looks new." "Nigga everything is the same you just haven't seen it in a while." "Yeah maybe you're right" Jaquan said. With that thought he laid back and put in a CD, which was Dipset and blasted the music. Sheena let it blast for a few seconds then turned it completely down and said, "You all mines today and tonight so don't think you'll be showing your face around town to these nothing ass niggas and bitches." "Now why would you think that", said Jaquan. "Cause I know how you do! You don't need anything from nobody; they didn't do nothing for us when you was down, so no need to have they phony Asses around now." "You know what, your right so I just

Gotta respect that." "Yeah you have no choice" then she blasted the music up again to kill the subject.

As Sheena switched lanes to get off on exit 28 on route 9 she thought about what Jaquan was going to wear. All the clothes she had of his were way too small now. "Bay what size you wear now with your diesel ass?" "Maybe a 42-44 in pants, ten and a half in shoes, and maybe a 2x or 3x it depends on how the shit is made", said Jaquan. "Don't worry about nothing my love I'm a fix you up real nice cause right now you look like a jail bird." Jaquan smiled and said "Yeah but you look like a young ass midget with a fucked up wig that you stole from your grandmother." Sheena and Jaquan busted out laughing with that joke. She loved him for that; he could always put a smile on her face regardless if she was mad or not. She had been with Jaquan for 10 years already and wasn't planning on leaving on him.

Sheena was five feet 6 inches one hundred eighty five pounds with a wine glass shape. She kept her hair short in style so it would be easy to do. Sheena got off the exit and pulled in the New Britain plaza to do some quick shopping. She could see the look on his face that he was still surprised to be home after so long. They walked into City Blues to buy three outfits and some sneakers. Sheena watched him pick out what he wanted.

The sound of the bells jingled as new customers walked through the doors. Jaquan turned toward the people who just walked in the store to recognize a familiar face. He then turned around trying to figure out where he knew the guy from. It was kind of hard at first until one of the three guys called a name

Yayo to look at a new pair of Jordan's that just came out. With that he remembered. He uses to hang with him back in school. His real name was Raymond Torres. Jaquan made his way down the same aisle to face them. He poked out his chest and then greeted, "What's popping Ray." Yayo looked at the man standing in front of him now. He starred with a grin then hugged Jaquan as soon as he recognized his baby face. "Damn nigga you got big as fuck, what the fuck you training for, the Olympics." They all started laughing then Jaquan said,

"Nah I got out of prison." "Yo these are my cousins Ed and Tiny" said Yayo. They all shook hands with respect.

Yayo was a short Puerto-Rican that came from New York. Him and Jaquan use to smoke weed before school and then go talking to every female they seen. That was the everyday routine back then but each one grew they own way. That's how Jaquan met Sheena. "Yo homie take my number down so we can get up sometime," said Yayo. "You know how we used to kick it back in the days. I see wifey coming so I'm a let you go. As soon as Yayo turned around Jaquan was looking at Sheena knowing she was about to make a fuss. "So you think you're real slick" said Sheena. "I'm not playing with you don't think you're gonna be hanging out getting into bullshit already. I'm the one who waited for you all this time so now I need my dick all day every day. Now let's hurry up so I can wash you up and feed you," said Sheena. "Okay whatever you say boss."

Sheena had plans for him; little did he know. She wanted to sex him a few times before his family came over her house and took all the attention from her. She wanted him all to herself, but she knew it would be hard. As soon as they got in the house her sister Candice was pulling the baked chicken out the oven. It was a lot of food on the table and kitchen counters. Jaquan smelled barber-Q chicken, collard greens, yams, cornbread, and rice and beans. By the way things looked he thought it was Thanksgiving. Candice ran and hugged

Jaquan, happy to see him. "Oh my God K-Lou you got so big", said Candice. "Shit you're the one who got all big. When I went to jail you were a little girl, now you're all grown now". Baby what the hell is in the water? Sheena smiled and said, "It's not in the water it just runs in the family". Candice called Jaquan K-Lou because that was his street name. K was for killer and Lou was for his middle name. He was amazed how Candice filled out. They both had sexy bodies but, she was a baby back then. He was starting to realize shit was going to be different because people grew up and got into different things in life. Candice now 18 years old looked like a model. He stared at her for a moment then said to Sheena, "Bay get me a towel and rag so I can get this jail smell off of me." "Say no more", she said and Jaquan walked towards the shower.

Available on www.LuLu.com

URBAN FICTION NOVEL

These Bad Bitches Be Side-Chick's

BY: Troy G-Five Hough

COMING SOON

COMING SOON

COMING SOON

COMING SOON

COMING SOON

SOUL SNATCHERZ

BY: Troy G-Five Hough

COMING SOON

COMING SOON

COMING SOON

COMING SOON

www.ingramcontent.com/pod-product-compliance
Lightning Source LLC
Chambersburg PA
CBHW020004050426
42450CB00005B/299